So, You Want to Be a
to Be a
Coder?

So, You Want to Be a Coder?

<The Ultimate Guide to a Career in Programming, Video Game Creation, Robotics, and More!/>

Jane (J.M.) Bedell

BE WHAT YOU WANT series

ALADDIN
New York London Toronto Sydney New Delhi

BEYOND WORDS
Hillsboro, Oregon

ALADDIN
An imprint of Simon & Schuster
Children's Publishing Division
1230 Avenue of the Americas
New York, NY 10020

BEYOND WORDS
20827 N.W. Cornell Road, Suite 500
Hillsboro, Oregon 97124-9808
503-531-8700 / 503-531-8773 fax
www.beyondword.com

This Beyond Words/Aladdin edition May 2016

For information about special discounts for bulk purchases, please contact
Simon & Schuster Special Sales at 1-866-506-1949 or business@simonandschuster.com.
The Simon & Schuster Speakers Bureau can bring authors to your live event.

For more information or to book an event contact the Simon & Schuster Speakers Bureau
at 1-866-248-3049 or visit our website at www.simonspeakers.com.

Managing Editor: Lindsay S. Easterbrooks-Brown
Editors: Emmalisa Sparrow, Kristin Thiel
Design: Sara E. Blum
Composition: William H. Brunson Typography Services
The text of this book was set in Bembo STD.

Manufactured in the United States of America 0416 FFG

10 9 8 7 6 5 4 3 2 1

Library of Congress Cataloging-in-Publication Data

Names: Bedell, J. M. (Jane M.), author.
Title: So, you want to be a coder? : the ultimate guide to a career in programming,
  video game creation, robotics, and more! / Jane (J. M.) Bedell.
Other titles: Be what you want series.
Description: New York : Aladdin, [2016] | Series: Be what you want series |
  Audience: Ages 10-12. | Audience: Grades 4 to 6. | Includes
  bibliographical references.
Identifiers: LCCN 2015040640 (print) | LCCN 2015044755 (ebook) |
  ISBN 9781582705798 (pbk.) | ISBN 9781582705804 (hardcover) |
  ISBN 9781481460637 (eBook)
Subjects: LCSH: Computer programming—Juvenile literature. | Computer
  programming—Vocational guide—Juvenile literature. | Programming
  languages (Electronic computers)—Juvenile literature.
Classification: LCC QA76.6 .B426 2016 (print) | LCC QA76.6 (ebook) |
  DDC 005.1023—dc23
LC record available at http://lccn.loc.gov/2015040640

If we want America to stay on the cutting edge, we need young Americans like you to master the tools and technology that will change the way we do just about everything.

—BARACK OBAMA, FIRST AMERICAN PRESIDENT TO WRITE CODE

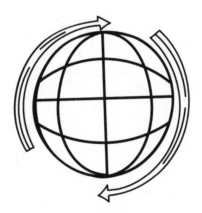

CONTENTS

Entering a Coding Career

Question: How do you define *hardware*?

ANSWER: IT'S THE PART OF A COMPUTER THAT YOU CAN KICK!

Congratulations! You made an excellent choice. You picked up and opened a book that I hope will introduce you to a career that is exciting and challenging. And well paid too!

When you think about writing code, you probably dream about designing an action-packed video game riddled with warriors, heroes, monsters, or trolls; building a robot that can walk the dog and take out the trash; or developing the machines that will put a human colony on Mars. Any one of these dreams is within your grasp if you decide that becoming a programmer is the right career for you.

Today, a large part of our world is built on code. From the first computers that could add and subtract numbers, to the code that directed the Philae lander to set down on a comet that was flying at eleven thousand miles per hour through space, the people who write computer code are the driving force behind new innovations around the world.

In our internet age, every company from food producers to sportswear manufacturers is a technical company. Businesses need websites to promote their products. Banks need new ways to protect their customers' business transactions. Governments need help organizing all the information that comes to them each day. And everyone wants their identities protected, their packages delivered fast, and their movies streaming without a glitch.

> There are toy race cars that use artificial intelligence to compete without drivers! With no tracks and no one at the controls, these cars sense what your car is doing, think for themselves, and race against you. Anki cofounder and CEO Boris Sofman said about the Drive cars, "They sense the environment five hundred times per second. They have fifty megahertz computers inside of them. They understand where they are and they communicate."[1]

What career links all of these needs? You guessed it! Coding. And because the demand for coders is growing fast, there aren't enough talented, trained people to fill the need. That's where you fit in. If this is the right career for you, the jobs are out there, waiting to be filled.

Five Traits You Need to Succeed as a Coder

Entering the world of coding begins with an understanding of what it takes to be a coder or computer programmer. As a coder, you should love to solve problems, revel in discovering new ways of doing things, and question everything. You must be a good listener and know how to manage your time. Here are a few important traits that every programmer needs.

<Courage/>
If you look at a line of code and are scared because you don't understand it, have courage! You aren't alone. Like learning any new

language, you start with the basics and build on that knowledge until you can speak and write it fluently. Courage will help you put your fears aside and embrace the trial-and-error process essential to learning any new skill.

<Creativity/>

You are a creative being. If your creative side leans toward solving problems and looking at things in unique and different ways, programming might be right for you. When writing code, there are many different ways to solve a problem and get the job done. If you love to tackle problems and find solutions, you can use your talent to produce efficient, graceful, and easy-to-maintain programs.

In 1949, *Popular Mechanics* predicted, "Where a calculator like ENIAC today is equipped with 18,000 vacuum tubes and weighs 30 tons, computers in the future may have only 1,000 vacuum tubes and perhaps weigh only one 1 ½ tons."[2] What they couldn't predict was the invention of the transistor and the integrated circuit, which both drastically shrunk the size of a computer.

<Logic/>

Make no mistake. You must be able to think logically to work as a coder. Computers follow basic rules of logic in order to do their job, so good coders are logical thinkers. They approach each problem with one thought in mind: there is a solution; I just have to find it. To do that, they break a problem down into smaller pieces, and by following a set of programming rules, they build and rebuild their program until the problem is solved.

<Passion/>

Most programmers are engineers at heart. You need to be passionate about building things, taking things apart, questioning processes, and solving problems. Coders' passion for discovery can leave others bewildered. But it is passion that keeps them working late into the night and on weekends while others play golf or stroll along the beach. Without passion, the process of learning and writing code could become overwhelming.

<Patience/>

Patience is what is needed to overcome the difficulty of learning a computer language. If you aren't patient, your desire to learn will quickly fade. Like learning to play a musical instrument or write a good story, patience is necessary for success. Even when passion fades and frustration sets in, patience will carry you through.

Computer, the Word

In 1613, the word *computer* entered the English lexicon. It was borrowed from the French word *compute*, which in turn was borrowed from the Latin word *computare*, which means "to count, sum up; to reckon."

Originally, the word *computer* was used to describe a person who worked with numbers. Then, sometime in the late 1800s, machines began to do the number-crunching work faster and more accurately than any person. The word quickly moved from describing a person to describing a machine.

\<Spotlight/\>

Charles Babbage (1791–1871), Father of Computing

Charles Babbage was born in England on December 26, 1791. When Charles was around eight years old, he became deathly ill with a fever. To aid in his recovery, his parents sent him to study in southern England, but his continuing poor health forced him to return home to be privately tutored.

Under the guidance of his tutors, Babbage studied many subjects, including continental mathematics and algebra. In 1811, he entered Trinity College. While at Trinity, he cofounded the Analytical Society, which promoted continental mathematics and worked to steer the college away from teaching Newtonian mathematics, which was the popular theory at the time.

In 1816, he was elected into the Royal Society of London, a society for those who contributed to the improvement of knowledge in mathematics, engineering science, and medical science. In 1820, he helped found the Royal Astronomical Society.

Babbage's Difference Engine, invented in 1821, was the first machine that could perform simple mathematical tasks with speed and accuracy. With the help of government funding, he built the machine, and when it was finished, it became the first successful automatic calculator. Unfortunately, his funding ended in 1832, and a decade later, the government ended the project.

After the Difference Engine, Babbage devoted his time and his fortune to designing an even better machine, the Analytical Engine. This machine could perform not just one mathematical task, but any kind of mathematical calculation. The Analytical Engine was never completed, but it had elements in common with today's computers.

From 1828 to 1839, Babbage was the Lucasian Chair of Mathematics at the University of Cambridge. He helped establish the Royal Statistical Society and lobbied the government and influential members of society to invest in the study of mathematics and science.

Today, little remains of Babbage's prototype computing machines. In 1991, the Science Museum in London finished construction of Difference Engine No. 2, using Babbage's original designs. The device, on display at the museum, consists of four thousand parts and weighs over three metric tons.

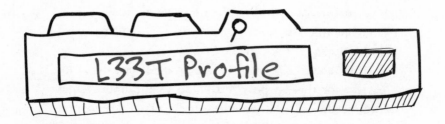

Name: Kelly Clarke
Job: Software engineer, NASA Jet Propulsion Laboratory

When did you first become interested in writing computer code and decide to make it the focus of your career?
In the seventh grade. My homeroom classroom had computers in it—which was a new thing in the late 1980s. I was able to sign up for an elective course that taught Logo (a computer language), and I remember working on a program to write my name on the screen in cursive. Later, I chose to be bused across town to William C. Overfelt High School in San Jose because it had a magnet program using computers. I had to convince my parents to let

me go, but it turned out that the school had amazing teachers, some I'm still friends with today. I learned BASIC and Pascal. At UC Berkeley, I chose to major in computer science for my bachelor's. I used Assembly, C, C++, and the like. I graduated in 1996 during the technology boom and then went to work for Hewlett-Packard.

What education/work path did you take to get to your current position at NASA?

I was working at Hewlett-Packard's spin-off, Agilent Technologies, when, in 2000, my husband heard about a career fair at the Jet Propulsion Laboratory (JPL). A section manager at the laboratory circulated my résumé, and I got several interviews.

What helped me the most, besides the section manager passing out my résumé, was my answer to one question asked at the career fair: What is your favorite programming language? My answer was that it depended entirely on the task at hand. If it was a short little tool to solve a simple problem, using a shell [batch file script] or Perl is going to be easier. If it's a large team effort for a large tool that would be maintained for years, C++ or Java would be easier.

Languages can be taught. The things that can't be taught as easily are the ability to think and a person's attitude.

What does an average workday look like for you?

At HP/Agilent, it was almost all software coding, with occasional meetings.

It has varied over my career at JPL. When I first started, I did a little bit of user support and troubleshooting, but most of my time was spent designing, coding, or talking to people about coding (from peer reviews to design reviews to testing to development techniques). Not long after I started, I became the cognizant engineer over the Mission Control and Analysis subsystem—which had many tools in it written in various languages. Being the cognizant engineer meant the buck stopped with me—I had to answer any and all questions about this area at any time.

However, I found over time I gravitated toward the operations side, actually using the software in the environments they were designed for. I just found it more fun. As that happened, I did less coding and more figuring out what is actually needed by the end users and communicating that to the software developers.

Now I'm splitting my job between two hats, one is a manager, where I spend most of my time in meetings. Since it involves areas such as ground software test, integration, and deployment, there are lots of people I need to bring together, and technical and process items to work and evolve. The software is meant to be used by all of NASA's robotic missions, not just JPL's.

I'm leaving this manager role and transitioning to a role with the Europa mission. Europa is an icy moon of Jupiter which may harbor life. I'm leading the Europa ground-system software team and will be working with others to ensure we develop all the software here on Earth that we will need to communicate to and from the spacecraft and provide tools for the spacecraft team to analyze all the data it sends.

What was your involvement in the Cassini-Huygens mission?

I started working on Cassini-Huygens my first day at JPL in 2000. Cassini had already been launched in 1997, and at the end of December 2000, it flew by Jupiter. I also supported Cassini in July 2004 when it entered Saturn's orbit. The Hugyen's probe separated from Cassini on December 25, 2004, and Hugyen's landed January 14, 2005.

Even though I supported those mission-critical activities, I did more behind-the-scenes support. I helped the mission's test facilities out—Integration Test Laboratory—where command sequences were sent to be verified prior to going to the real space-craft. I adapted software, wrote small software tools, hooked up existing tools, automated software. All of it centered on uplink-ing commands to the test spacecraft or downlinking data from it.

Explain the Mars Exploration Rover and your involvement with it.

I joined the Mars Exploration Rovers in 2003, after they had launched and were en route to Mars. They were named Spirit and Opportunity. I worked to help ensure that the data could be seen from the spacecraft by all the team members.

When Spirit landed on January 4, 2004, I was working in the room right behind the cameras filming the event. We went through the "seven minutes of terror," waiting for the spacecraft to land. It was intense! For the actual event, I went into the camera room and jumped up and down with the team, and came right back out to get back to work.

A few days before Opportunity was set to land, Spirit had an anomaly. I was on shift that night, when Spirit stopped talking back to Earth. It took some time, but we figured out that she wasn't going to sleep, and she was wasting her battery. We were at risk of losing the mission. Eventually, the team managed to get her to a safe state from which she could be recovered.

Opportunity landed January 25, 2004. Each rover was supposed to last on Mars for ninety sols (ninety Martian days), which was their primary mission. It was thought that they may go a little longer, but eventually their solar panels would be covered in dust, and there would not be enough power to keep the instruments and the rovers themselves warm and alive (Mars is very cold!). Luckily, the Martian winds put dust on the solar panels, but they also take it off. This was a happy surprise to everyone. Spirit was stuck with wheel issues, and we could not get her into a good position for the solar arrays (sun and wind). She was last heard from on March 22, 2010—about six years longer than we expected her to work. Opportunity is still going today (May 1, 2015) with over four thousand sols on Mars and over a marathon in driving.

For Spirit and Opportunity, I did primarily operations—using the software others had created and running it, troubleshooting issues, even performing as a help desk for data- and software-related issues.

I stopped working on Spirit and Opportunity not long after ninety sols for a few reasons. The team had been working around the clock (twenty-four hours a day, seven days a week) for the entire ninety sols. The team went slowly to more human-friendly Earth hours. Our team worked around the clock on

Earth time; most other teams actually shifted with Mars time, which meant coming in about forty minutes later each day. So they needed fewer people. And I needed to get back to Cassini-Huygens because Cassini was soon to get to a mission-critical event—Saturn Orbit Insertion.

What part did you play in the Curiosity Rover mission?
I was very briefly back working on the still-going Spirit and Opportunity Rovers before I moved on to the Mars Science Laboratory—later renamed Curiosity. Curiosity was both an amazing rover and an amazing journey for me. One of the highlights of working on Curiosity for me was working in the teams that supported the building, launching, and landing of Curiosity.

For launch, I was in the room. I had to say, "Go" or "No go," depending on if the ground software (software here on Earth) was ready for the launch or not. I gave the go. We had to watch our monitors until about T-30 seconds, when the person in charge gave the go-ahead for myself and others to run outside (we were at Kennedy Space Center in Florida) and watch the launch. Two persons waited until T-10 seconds. It was awesome to see something I'd worked closely with the past four years take off from our home planet! I thought I'd see nothing as cool as that launch on November 26, 2011.

I was wrong. Curiosity's cruise to Mars was also a busy time. We practiced the landing on Mars many times, and not one of the practice landings for the team went perfectly right! I had multiple teams I had to oversee, including the team that ran the uplink/downlink software and the team that sent commands to Curiosity.

On landing night, August 5, 2012, Pacific Time about 10:30 PM, it was dramatic. The seven minutes of terror were way scarier for me than they had been on Spirit and Opportunity. The landing mechanisms had to be far different because of the size of Curiosity, and I had spent five years instead of five months working on the mission. I had worked to ensure everything possible had been done beforehand, but that night there were still items we had to do. We expected huge numbers of people to log in to watch—we got even more. Curiosity went beyond the point of no return—she had landed, one way or another (success or crash) on Mars—we just didn't know yet. I was ecstatic when we landed successfully! All the systems and teams I had helped set up worked perfectly, and we displayed the first black-and-white images of Curiosity—with wheels down on Mars—and even a plume from where the descent stage had safely crashed far away from the Rover. A highlight of my life.

All in all, an amazing journey. And it continues. Next stop: Europa!

What were the most exciting moments for you during your career at NASA?

1. Curiosity's landing—I still get goose bumps thinking about it.

2. Spirit's landing

3. Opportunity's landing

4. Curiosity's launch

5. Hugyen's landing on Europa

What is it like for you as a female programmer in a male-dominated career?

I was surrounded by men in college. One of my classes had ninety-four of us for the main lecture, and only four of us were female.

At JPL, it's been both ways. For example, on the rover missions, a good number of people building the rover (electrically) and the landing team were male. However, there were many females in ground software, and the planners and mission team for surface operations may have more females than males!

I've been in meetings that have been dominated by one gender—both ways. At JPL, being female has never been an issue. New hires and senior personnel, as well as males and females, are all listened to whenever anybody has an idea or concern. Everyone has the same goal: make this spacecraft work so the scientists can get their data and expand mankind's knowledge of our universe.

What do you see in the future for computer programming, at NASA or in general?

The cybersecurity environment is changing the nature of the way we do business. Instead of adding security as an afterthought, security needs to be designed into the architecture of every software program from day zero.

Do you have any tips for kids who are interested in becoming programmers?

What programming languages you know sometimes matters and sometimes doesn't. Now that search algorithms for résumés do pattern matching, having some experience with a particular language can help get your résumé into the right hands. In my opinion, critical thinking is more important than languages. For example, do you understand what design can meet the user's need?

By far the most important skills are the hardest to teach: the ability to work well with others as partners on the same software program and listening to and understanding the customer's needs. Also, seize opportunities to try out your programming in the real world with internships, summer jobs, or other opportunities. There are many areas and types of software engineering. It's good to find out which kind you do or do not like when it's applied to the real world before you enter it full-time. Enjoy what you do; do what you enjoy!

0100100100100100100100100100100100100100010

History of the Computer

50,000 BCE: The first evidence of counting can be dated all the way back to this year.

30,000 BCE: Evidence of recording numbers by putting notches on bone, ivory, or stone remains from as far back as this time.

300 BCE: People create what is now the oldest known abacus, called the Salamis Tablet. The abacus is a calculating tool that is still in use today.

150–100 BCE: Greeks create the Antikythera Mechanism, an ancient computer used to predict eclipses and planet positions.

1623: Wilhelm Schickard builds the first automatic, nonprogrammable calculator, which he calls the calculating clock.

1642: Frances Pascal invents a machine that can add, subtract, and carry digits.

1679: Gottfried Leibniz discovers binary arithmetic that shows that every number can be represented by using only 0s and 1s.

1820: Charles de Colmar invents the first reliable, commercially successful, mechanical calculating machine called the Arithometer.

1837: Charles Babbage designs the Analytical Engine, the first computer to use punch cards as memory.

1842: Ada Lovelace develops the first computer code, an algorithm, or list of instructions, to be processed by a machine.

1889: Herman Hollerith describes the first electric tabulating machine and proves that data can be encoded on punch cards and then counted and sorted electronically.

1903: Nikola Tesla patents electrical logic circuits called gates or switches.

1932: ROM-type storage media is introduced. Read-only memory is later used in the start-up process of a computer.

1936: Konrad Zuse creates the Z1, the first binary digital computer controlled using punch tape.

Paul Eisler invents the printed circuit board, the precursor to today's computer motherboard.

1937: John Atanasoff, with help from graduate student Clifford Berry, creates the first electronic digital computer, the Atanasoff–Berry computer (ABC), at Iowa State College.

1940: George Stibitz presents a complex calculator at Dartmouth College and demonstrates, for the first time, remote–access computing.

1943: Tommy Flowers develops the first electric programmable computer, named Colossus, to solve encrypted German messages during World War II.

1945: John von Neumann defines a stored-program computer. His idea of electronic storage of information transforms the development of the modern computer.

1946: Konrad Zuse writes the first algorithmic, or instruction list, programming language, called Plankalkül or Plan Calculus.

1947: On December 23, the transistor is born at Bell Laboratory. The transistor is an important invention of the electronic age.

1949: Maurice Wilkes assembles the first computer capable of storing and running a program from memory. He also creates the first library of short programs, called subroutines, and stores them on punched paper tapes.

1952: Alexander Douglas designs the first graphical-display computer game, which is a version of tic-tac-toe.

1954: IBM sells its first mass-produced computer, the 650 Magnetic Drum Calculator. It sells 450 in one year.

1955: The Whirlwind machine is the first digital computer with real-time graphics and magnetic core RAM (random-access memory). Also, the first transistor computer is introduced. It is smaller, faster, and more reliable than previous computers.

1960: Two thousand computers are in use in the United States.

1962: Three Massachusetts Institute of Technology (MIT) students create SpaceWar!, the first shooter-style game for computers.

1967: Floppy disks are used to install programs and back up information.

Wally Feurzeig and Seymour Papert create Logo, the first programming language for children, designed to help solve simple problems through play.

1968: Hewlett Packard starts selling the HP 9100A, the first mass-marketed, desktop, personal computer.

1971: Intel introduces the first microprocessor.

The first email is sent.

The first speech-recognition program is introduced.

1975: Bill Gates and Paul Allen start Microsoft.

1975: IBM releases the first portable computer. It weighs fifty-five pounds, has a five-inch display, and has 64 KB of RAM.

1979: Over five hundred thousand computers are in use in the United States.

The Mother of All Demos

On December 9, 1968, Douglas Engelbart introduced a fully functioning online workstation at the Fall Joint Computer Conference in San Francisco. His ninety-minute presentation held one thousand computer experts spellbound!

He demonstrated new ideas like windows, menus, icons, graphics, shared-screen collaboration using audio and video, file linking, hypertext, object addressing, word processing with revision control and a real-time editor, and the computer mouse. This was the first time all of these fundamental elements of the modern computer were demonstrated to the public on a single system.

Engelbart's demonstration influenced the design of the Xerox Alto in the 1970s, which in turn influenced the Apple Macintosh computers and the Microsoft Windows graphical user interface operating systems of the '80s and '90s. Almost fifty years later, Engelbart's demonstration is still considered the most important event in computer history.

1981: The first US patent for a computer software program is approved.

1982: The first compact disk for storage is invented in Germany.

1983: Over ten million computers are in use in the United States.

1986: The first laptop computer, IBM's PC Convertible, is announced. It weighs twelve pounds.

1994: IBM introduces the first notebook with a CD-ROM, the ThinkPad 775CD.

2007: Apple introduces the iPhone.

2010: Apple introduces the iPad.

2012: Raspberry Pi, a small, cheap, credit card–size computer that plugs into a monitor or television and uses a standard keyboard and mouse is introduced. It is designed to help teach computer programming in languages like Scratch and Python.

There are over 310 million personal computers in use in the United States.

Name: Karel the Dog
Age: 3
Job: Coding enthusiast and CodeHS mascot

When did you first become interested in helping kids learn to write code?

I got into coding at a very early age, when I learned to move. Then I saw I could help others do the same, and I've been helping ever since then. So it's pretty much been my whole life!

How did you become the main character in a computer program?

You know, that's a tough one. I was programmed in by someone else, maybe Jeremy or one of his friends? But it always makes me wonder if I'm the only one. Maybe we are all living in a simulation.

You and your friend Jeremy Keeshin, cofounder of CodeHS, go on road trips to teach kids how to write

code. How did you get started traveling, and why is it important to you?

We started traveling about two years ago. I think it's really important to meet the different students and teachers who are learning coding with CodeHS. By visiting all the classrooms, we can really help out. And because I'm cute and cuddly, the kids get interested real fast.

Describe some of the schools you visit.

Schools are different in so many ways. There are big schools and small schools. There are different types of schools. There are city schools and rural schools and home schools. I think one of the things that varied a lot and was really interesting was the culture and feel of the school. Some are very strict, and some let you do whatever you want. There are lots of ways to run a school! But every school is filled with amazing kids who love to code!

What do you enjoy most about teaching kids to write code?

I think the most exciting part is when someone gets that aha moment when they solve a problem. They get all excited and call me over to their computers to see what they did. That's an awesome, scratch-your-belly kind of moment for me.

You have a website, Karelthedog.com, where you document your travels. Describe some of the places you've visited.

We've been to almost every single state in the United States now except for Alaska. And I can't wait to go there, except I heard they have a lot of mosquitoes. I don't like mosquitoes. My favorite places we visited are New York City and Little Rock, Arkansas. I really like going to see Mount Rushmore, as well as Old Faithful in Yellowstone National Park. I also like traveling from place to place in the van. During those days, I get all of Jeremy's attention.

0100100100100100100100100100100100100100010010010

Quiz
Is Writing Code Right for Me?

1. Do you like solving puzzles?

    A. *I love solving puzzles. I play with them on my computer or mobile phone every chance I get. I find great satisfaction in solving really hard ones.*

    B. *I like puzzles and play with them once in a while. Sometimes I invite my friends to play with me. I enjoy the competition.*

    C. *I only enjoy puzzles when I have a group of my friends playing with me.*

2. When faced with a big homework assignment, I . . .

    A. *Break the assignment into smaller pieces and focus on one segment at a time.*

    B. *Do the fun parts first and finish the rest of the assignment as quickly as possible.*

    C. *Feel overwhelmed by big assignments and sometimes struggle to get it all done.*

3. Do you sweat the small stuff?

    A. *Sometimes I drive myself crazy, but I always notice even the smallest details.*

    B. *I notice details, but I'm really more of a big-picture person.*

    C. *Details? No, thanks—I don't like to let little things weigh me down.*

4. How important is accuracy to you?

  A. *I try to do things right the first time, but I always double-check my work, just in case.*

  B. *I don't mind going back and fixing my mistakes. Accuracy is important, but not at the expense of getting my ideas across.*

  C. *I like to be accurate, but isn't it overrated? Focusing too much on accuracy stifles my creativity.*

5. You spend three days working on a project, and the first time you use what you made, it breaks. You . . .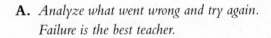

  A. *Analyze what went wrong and try again. Failure is the best teacher.*

  B. *Restart the project from the beginning. Those three days were a waste!*

  C. *Take the project to a group of friends and see if they can help.*

6. Do you like working with computers?

  A. *Yes! I'm constantly on one.*

  B. *Sometimes. I find them a useful tool.*

  C. *I use them only when I have to.*

7. How do you feel about spending hundreds of hours learning how to write a computer program?

  A. *I already have a list of the colleges with the best computer science programs. I can't wait!*

  B. *I would prefer to learn computer coding on my own or take a technical class.*

  C. *I think it sounds tedious.*

8. How do you interact with other people?

   A. *I like to work alone, but I understand the need to get along with others and work as a team.*

   B. *I can work alone, but I'd rather work with others and build consensus.*

   C. *I am happiest when I'm working with other people.*

Answers:

If you answered mostly As: Keep pursuing a career as a computer programmer.

If you answered mostly Bs: You could succeed as a programmer but keep an open mind about working in other areas of the computer sciences.

If you answered mostly Cs: Look into working in areas of computer science where you can use the computer but don't have to write the software.

Getting a Coding Education

Question: What do you call a programmer from
Scandinavia?

ANSWER: A NERDIC.

In 2014, England introduced computer programming classes into every grade in every public school in the country. Starting at age five, students are gradually introduced to the logic and reasoning skills needed to write a useful computer program. Educators there feel that understanding the principles behind what makes a computer work is essential for any worker in the twenty-first century, which is how they view learning a new language or a musical instrument as well.

Is the United States falling behind? Many would say that the answer is a resounding yes! Only 10 percent of the high schools in the United States teach advanced placement computer science to their students. According to the Bureau of Labor Statistics and Code.org, by 2020, there will be one million more computing jobs than students to fill them.[1] If the state school systems don't recognize the need, thousands and thousands of well-paying jobs will be lost to other countries and their workers.

What does this mean to you? Do the work; get the training. There will be a job waiting for you when you are ready.

Robots Rule! This is what many young programmers and engineers think when they enter the RoboCup International Competition. The coolest robots so far? The ones that play soccer on two legs. Now that's a mechanical and computer programming feat. The ultimate goal? To create robots that can play against humans and win the FIFA World Cup in 2050.

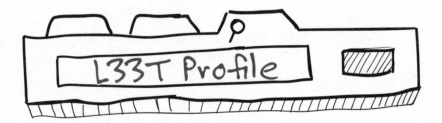

Name: Louise D. Stinnett
Job: Senior systems programmer and analyst (retired), Coorman-Douglas Corporation

When did you first become interested in writing computer code and decide to make it the focus of your career? In the mid-1960s, I was working for an insurance company as an actuary clerk. That's a person who uses math, statistics, and other information to help insurance companies decide how much risk there is in issuing different types of policies. One day, my coworkers and I were in the office chatting during the lunch hour. Our boss came in and tricked us into taking an aptitude test for computer programming. Fortunately for me, I scored very high on the test and soon found myself learning how to program using Fortran. Fortran is a computer language that works well for math-based applications.

Hour of Code

Some educators are seeing the need and demanding that kids learn to code. Not because everyone will become a professional coder, but because everyone will be impacted by computer code in their future careers.

In an effort to jump-start this learning process, code.org sponsors an Hour of Code. They ask teachers to organize one hour of computer coding for their students, using the tools available on the organizaton's website. Their hope is that by explaining code writing to teachers, parents, and government decision makers, they can begin to understand the importance of teaching coding to children.

During the 2014 Hour of Code event, about fifteen million students participated. Since its inception, Hour of Code has reached tens of millions of students, 48 percent of them female, in over 180 countries.

Hour of Code events are held each year during Computer Science Education Week in early December. The date was chosen to honor the birthday of computing pioneer Admiral Grace Hopper, whose birth date was December 9, 1906.

I wrote programs that saved a lot of time and saved my company a lot of money. Before my programs, we could spend days using a calculator to solve problems. After my programs, the computations took only minutes to do. Shortly after that, I got a trainee position in the data-processing department.

What education/work path did you take before you started programming?

I started out working toward a career in account-ing. When I entered the programmer training program, there were no formal classes. IBM set up a series of classes and came to our office to teach us. It was a very thorough series, and we learned a lot.

You began programming in the 1960s. What programming languages did you use?

I originally coded using Fortran. The next languages were COBOL (Common Business-Oriented Language) and JCL (Job Control Language). When I first started coding using the COBOL language, we were limited to 28K. So when storage got tight, we had to count the bytes of any new instructions and changes. Some instructions were flagged as *Do Not Use* because they generated too many bytes!

What was it like to write code in the 1960s?

The computer room was huge and filled with large machines. There were disk drives, tape drives, card readers, card punchers, and control units. The key-punch opera-tors would punch our original code, but if we had to make any corrections, we had to punch them up on cards ourselves.

At one point in time, there were disk drives that had removable disks the size of dinner plates! They came in a pack of five or more. One night, an operator didn't put the pack into the drive cor-rectly. You could hear the screech of the needles against the disks throughout the entire building. The drive and the disk pack were ruined. An expensive mistake to make.

By the time I had a program coded and tested, it consisted of a huge number of cards that were placed in a tray. We were sup-posed to number the cards, so if something happened, we could put them back in the proper order. Unfortunately, writing a number on every card was tedious, and sometimes we didn't do it. Instead, we would take a marker and draw a line across the top of the pack of cards from the upper left corner to the lower right corner. Against our boss' advice, we often did this.

One day, I was carrying a two-foot tray and dropped it. There were cards everywhere! It took me several days to get the cards back in order. Needless to say, I learned my lesson and did a permanent update, so my coding wasn't lost again. In those days, an update took about a week, something that today takes only minutes.

What was it like to be a female coder in the 1960s?
In the 1960s, companies could pick a man for a job over a woman, regardless of their qualifications. The trainer position I got was one out of three available positions. The company decided it was going to pick two men and one woman, regardless of anyone's test scores. There were twenty-eight people who applied for those three positions. Twenty of them were female and eight were male. Luckily for me, I had the top test scores. Luckily for women today, this can't happen anymore. There are laws in place to prevent it.

Companies could also pay men more than women and promote them over women, no matter how hard the woman worked. At one point, my company wanted me to train a man to take over the section I was in rather than give me the job. I had to train him, and then he got the job and the pay raise!

What did you enjoy most and least about writing code?
The most enjoyable part was when I got to solve problems and come up with creative solutions. The part I hated most was trying to find errors that were nothing more than a missing period!

0100100100100100100100100100100100100010010

<Spotlight/>

Sister Mary Kenneth Keller (1914–1985), First Woman to Receive a PhD in Computer Science

Sister Mary Kenneth Keller was born around 1914. Although little is known about her early life in Ohio, by the age of eighteen, she had entered a Catholic religious order. She lived with the Sisters of Charity of the Blessed Virgin Mary and took her vows when she was twenty-six years old.

Keller attended DePaul University in Chicago and earned a bachelor's degree in mathematics and a master's degree in mathematics and physics. During her time as a graduate student, she studied at several schools, including Purdue University, the University of Michigan, and Dartmouth College. When she went to Dartmouth, it was still a men's-only college. But for her, the school broke with tradition and let her work in their computer center. While there, she helped develop the Beginner's All-purpose Symbolic Instruction Code (BASIC) programming language.

Later in life, when she was over fifty years old, she received her PhD in computer science from the University of Wisconsin–Madison. She was the first woman in America to earn that degree. After graduation, she took a teaching position at Clarke College in Iowa. While there, she started that college's computer applications in education master's degree program. She also founded their computer science department and was its leader for twenty years.

Keller was always interested in artificial intelligence and the future of computers. She once said, "For the first time, we can now mechanically simulate the cognitive process.

We can make studies in artificial intelligence. Beyond that, this mechanism [the computer] can be used to assist humans in learning. As we are going to have more mature students in greater numbers as time goes on, this type of teaching will probably be increasingly important."[2] Keller wrote four books about computer science and was an unwavering support to women entering the field. She died on January 10, 1985, at the age of seventy-one.

Going the College Route: Associate of Science (AS), Bachelor of Science (BS), or Master of Science (MS) Degree

Getting a job with any employer will depend on that employer's specific needs and requirements. For some, an AS in computer science will get you an entry-level position. For most, however, a minimum of a BS is required to work as a programmer and an MS for more complex jobs. You might want to choose a college that is recognized for its math or IT (information technology) programs—it could give you a better chance at landing your dream job.

Every employer will be interested in your experience. Inexperienced programmers can be expensive for a company because they need mentoring and additional training, and they can make costly mistakes. Because of this, it is important that you hone your programming skills by participating in as many internships as possible while earning your degree. You never know when an internship might lead to a full-time job with the company or an even better job with a different company.

Explore Microsoft is a twelve-week summer internship program for college freshmen and sophomores. It is designed to give students exposure to a variety of careers paths, computing tools, and programming languages. The internship offers hands-on training and group project experiences. This is a great way to find mentors, network with working programmers, and understand the inner workings of Microsoft's programming community.

If you decide that going to college is right for you, here are a couple things to consider when choosing a program of study. First, what do you want your career to look like? Start your thinking process by asking yourself which of these questions you find the most interesting.

⇨ Why does that computer software work the way it does?

⇨ How does that computer software work?

⇨ What software would work best to solve a problem?

 Second, read the following descriptions to see if the question you chose matches your interests for a college major. Remember, every college and university defines these degree programs a bit differently. When in doubt, ask your school advisor to help you choose the best major for you.

Computer Science (CS) major: Students who major in computer science are interested in *why* things work the way they do. As a computer science graduate, you will know how to write code in several languages and have the skills needed to start a career as a coder. You will also understand how computer operating systems work and why computer code works the way it does. Graduates with this major go on to develop new technology.

Information Technology (IT) major: Students who major in information technology are interested in *how* things work the way they do. As an IT graduate, you will understand how computers work together in an office environment. You will know how to keep your company's systems and data safe and how to manage all the data that is created. While in school, you will learn basic programming skills, but you'll have to learn one or two programming languages on your own. Your future job won't focus on writing code. Graduates with this major help companies put their computers to good use.

Information Systems (IS) major: Students who major in information systems are interested in *what* is the best technology that will get the job done. Your course load will be similar to the IT major's, but with a focus on solving business problems. In some schools, there is only a brief introduction to coding, and the major may fall within a school's college of business. IS graduates see the big picture—what computer system is best for a company, what is the best way to handle a project, and what is the best way to manage employees. An IS degree does not lead to a career as a coder.

Different colleges have different names for their majors. Armed with the information above, you should go to a school advisor and make sure you are choosing the education path that fits your career goals.

Here are some other college majors you might see:

⇨ Computer Engineering

⇨ Data Communication Systems Technology

⇨ Game Design

⇨ Game Software Development

⇨ Information Systems Security

⇨ Mathematics

⇨ Software Development

⇨ Software Engineer

Going the Self-Taught Route

Self-taught coding can be a path to a programming career but not with a large company. To work for a large company without a degree, you will need years of experience. That's not impossible, however. To gain that experience, you must start out working freelance or for a small company where you can get a job by demonstrating your skills. From there, you build a portfolio of work that will convince a recruiter that you know your stuff. The recruiter, in turn, can open the doors to bigger companies and bigger paychecks.

Hackerspaces

Hackerspaces are sometimes called makerspaces. They are buildings (spaces) where people come together to create something, usually a project using computers. The focus of any hackerspace is left to the individuals in the group, but every member is expected to share their tools, equipment, ideas, and expertise. Each space is part classroom, part studio, and part workshop. Each location is different, but the idea is the same: share your space—share your passion.

The first hackerspace opened in 1981 in Berlin, Germany. Today, according to hackerspaces.org, there are 1,142 active hackerspaces worldwide with almost two hundred in the United States. Most hackerspaces charge a membership fee and some are nonprofit organizations.

Today, thanks to the internet, it is possible to learn how to write code from other programmers or through websites dedicated to teaching programming languages. With an easy online search, you can find many websites that offer free tutorials, for-a-fee intensive boot camp classes, or online classes through colleges or technical schools. Self-taught programmers often earn their living by selling

applications that they have written. You may also find entry-level jobs listed on sites like Craigslist.org, elance.com, or oDesk.com.

Whether you go to college or are self-taught, it is important to remember that programming is evolving at a very fast pace. The coders who stay satisfied with their career choice are the ones who embrace change and learn to quickly adapt to new technologies.

Get an Agent!
Is This the Future for Computer Coders?

In industries that require creativity, it seems that talented, inventive people are often exploited by those with money and power. In the early days of recorded music, musicians and singers were forced to sell their songs and sign away their rights to recording companies. Even when a song sold millions of copies, the artist didn't get any more money.

At the dawn of filmmaking, actors were required to sign multiyear contracts that didn't allow for renegotiation, even when the artist became a star or shows made the company enormous profits. And in early book publishing, hopeful authors often sold manuscripts for a set fee, never receiving more money even when their books sold thousands or hundreds of thousands of copies.

Michael Solomon of 10x Management, in a 2014 article for *The New Yorker*, said that he sees "the exact same trend emerging with the tech industry. A lot of things can go wrong when a person just signs on the dotted line."[3]

As talented computer coders start demanding pay equal to their contributions to companies, more and more technical talent agencies are emerging. In the near future, the tech giants may no longer determine a programmer's pay. It might be in the hands of an agent.

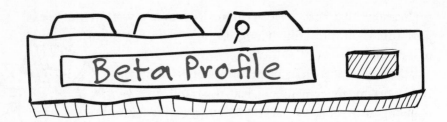

Name: Crystal Agerton
Age: 17
Job (when not studying!): President, Independence High School Coding Club

When did you first discover that you were interested in writing code?

I was introduced to coding during my sophomore year, through a webcomic called *Homestuck,* but I really became interested in the subject my junior year of high school in Mrs. Glazer's web design class.

How did you learn to write code, and what language(s) do you know?

Codecademy.com is where I learned HTML and where I am currently learning both Java and Python. I also learned some Java from CodeHS.com and other free sites that I experimented with.

Why did you decide to join a computer programming club?

The biggest reason for my decision to join IHS's Coding Club is that I was at the right place at the right time. I was there when it was suggested and created; plus I wanted to learn more about coding. The other part is actually so I could be like some of my favorite characters, who were expert coders, in *Homestuck.*

Describe your experiences in the club and as the club's president.

I started with the basics. Most of my first semester in the club I focused on learning HTML and starting with Java. During the second semester, we got into the LEGO Mindstorms project, where I worked with my friend Vananh to program LEGO robots to maneuver through obstacle courses. The Mindstorms project has probably been my favorite so far, since we actually got to see what our coding could translate to in real life. This past year, as president of the club, I've been acting more as a mentor for the newer members. I still work on improving my skills in Java and Python, but I try to focus more on the questions I'm asked. Besides coding, I'm learning better communication skills through this club.

Why is being a part of a coding club important?
Because it helps introduce a new field to students who may have never considered it before. Being a part of a coding club keeps people motivated and interested in coding. Without some sort of involvement, people have a tendency to drift away from things that initially interested them. As a club, it also helps students to meet and collaborate with people with similar interests, which could help them develop their skills as a coder and as a worker.

What led to your decision to pursue computer science at the University of California, Irvine, and what will be the focus of your studies?
Not knowing exactly what I wanted to do with my life beyond high school for years, I finally did some research into the computer science degree I was hearing so much about. Even after learning about it and all its applications in the workforce, I was uncertain. The summer before my senior year, I took an animation workshop for a couple days. That workshop solidified my desire to be in the animation business.

After researching animation-based careers, I discovered that a computer science degree was one of the requirements for some animation jobs. Between this evidence and my already being in a coding club, I decided to apply to colleges as a CS major. After getting all my acceptances and rejections, I was torn between UCI and UCSD [University of California, San Diego]. I finally decided on UCI because they had placed me in the CS program, unlike

UCSD. As for my focus, my current major is computer game science, so I will be studying the media side of computer science more than anything. However, I would like to learn more about robotics and [artificial] intelligence systems.

Why do you think it's important that your peers learn how to write code?
Considering the day and age we live in, and how much the internet and other technologies are becoming intrinsic in our lives, learning to code could be a job saver. Even if a job doesn't require knowing how to code, it could be beneficial to understanding how everything computer based around us runs and having the ability to converse about it when needed. After all, if you're going to be the inspiration, you should have some basic knowledge about what it will take to create your vision.

How do you balance your schoolwork with all your other activities?
That's the question I've been asking people since freshman year! It takes organization and good time-management skills. Those aren't easy skills to learn, I know, but learning how to balance everything is what high school is for.

Where do you see yourself in ten years?
In ten years, I see myself being successful. By that time, I would have finished college and obtained a well-paying job to pay for my comfortable house. I expect I would be working in the entertainment industry, possibly at Dreamworks or Disney or a gaming company, or working at a technological powerhouse like Google. Either way, I'll be happy, which is my main goal in life.

0100100100100100100100100100100100100100010

Certification

Certifications, given by recognized authorities, show that you have the skills needed to work with a specific computer language or have additional knowledge in a specific area like database management. For computer coders, here is a list of some of the most useful and recognized certifications.

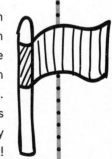

⇨ Adobe Certified Expert (ACE) for Developers

⇨ C/C++ Certificate

⇨ (ISC)2 Certified Secure Software Lifecycle Professional (CSSLP)

⇨ CompTia A+

⇨ GIAC Secure Software Programmer (GSSP-.NET) Certification

⇨ Google Apps for Business Certified Deployment Specialist (CDS)

⇨ Microsoft Certified Professional Developer (MCPD)

⇨ Oracle's Java Certification

International Programmers' Day

Programmers' Day began in 2007 as a way to honor computer programmers' contributions to society. The day is recognized in many countries, as well as within many technology and programming companies. Russia is the only country to officially observe the day.

The date of the celebration is always on the 256th day of the year, September 13, or September 12 on leap years. The 256th day was chosen because it is the number of distinct values that can be represented with an eight-bit byte, a value well-known to programmers. It is also the highest power of the number two that is less than 365, the number of days in a normal year. Only a computer programmer would choose a date like that!

Ten Keys to Becoming a Happy, Successful Coder

The world needs talented, happy coders! Every person who decides to write code is unique in his or her own very quirky, creative, and sometimes comical ways. To become a successful coder, you need to embrace and understand your own unique skills, passions, and personality. Beyond that, you need to understand what employers will expect from you. Here is some advice from Cory Miller, author of *Essential Career Advice for Developers*.[4] This list will help you hone the skills needed to succeed as you pursue your degree and enter the world of coding.

1. **Build your portfolio of cool projects that work.** Employers want to see stuff that shows you can actually do things with the skills you listed on your résumé. A good working project that solves a problem for users is one of the best ways to get a job. It demonstrates your skills, shows you can complete the work, and shows you have initiative.

2. **Get involved and contribute to an open source project.** Contributing to open source projects blends learning and networking, while also giving you a project to show. It's a triple win! Find a project that interests you, and get involved in the community around it. If you can't find one, release something cool you've built and build interest around your own project. Sharing on an open source project shows that you can work in a team.

3. **Value good communication skills almost as much as your programming skills.** Coders are brilliant, wonderful people, but let's face it—they aren't always the most social creatures. You may be able to code almost anything, but if you can't communicate with others, using their terms and language, you're going to struggle. Remember, communication is not the message sent but the message received. Memorize that. Work tirelessly on learning how

to communicate with the noncoding people of the world. Although communication is a two-way street, it's best if you work hard on your side of it. Here are some tips:

⇨ Be forever patient. Stay calm and always keep your composure.

⇨ Don't talk down to noncoding people. Remember that they aren't stupid—they just don't speak your language.

⇨ Translate for others. If you use a technical term, explain it. Seek out ways to compare your words to something in the listener's world. For example: A *database* is like a box filled with words, numbers, files, and phrases. A *database query* is how you choose what information to pull out of that box.

⇨ Restate what someone said to you. This is a good way to make sure you understand what is being said.

⇨ When all else fails, find a translator. Find one of those weird blends of people who can walk and talk in both the coding and the noncoding worlds. They are your allies. Keep one close by. Make him or her your workplace BFF.

4. **Finish the projects you start and ship them.** Code that never ships never has the chance to change the world. Shipping your code into the wild is extremely satisfying. You get to see if people care about it. You get to learn if you were right or wrong about the decisions and assumptions you made. Beware of perfectionism. It's a false goal that can kill your career. Other coders may judge your work, but while they are spewing hot air, you are learning and producing. Do good work; test, test, test; and then ship it!

5. **Park your arrogance at the door.** The best coders don't have to tell others that they are great. They let their *shipped* code speak for itself. Larger companies also perform code reviews. The code is inspected for correctness, completeness, and conformance to coding standards. You must be able to take criticism. Good coders are quietly

confident and park their egos at the door. Everyone loves a brilliant coder, but no one likes a show-off.

6. **Make sure you power down regularly.** Deadlines will always exist. The best coders learn how to schedule downtime and take it. Do something that forces you to leave your work behind and truly power down. Know yourself and the limits of your endurance. Read a novel, take a cooking class, play a musical instrument, or go snowboarding.

7. **Always be learning and exploring.** The best companies hire learners, people who seek out new things and try them. Learners are voracious readers. Expand your interests and study something you never thought you would like— you might be surprised. Learn and grow on your own time. Don't expect your boss to invest in your skills. Invest in yourself with books, conferences, training, webinars, classes, or online video training. Do what it takes to learn and grow.

8. **Pass it on.** As you progress in your coding, pass that knowledge on to others. Seek out ways to mentor, teach, train, or help someone who is in your circle of influence. Sharing with others is the sign of a good leader.

Looking at the Languages

Question: Why do Java programmers have to wear glasses?

ANSWER: BECAUSE THEY DON'T C#! (THEY DON'T "SEE SHARP"—
GET IT? GET IT?)

The first question you'll probably ask about computer languages is, Why can't I just write my program in English? The answer is because the English language is too vague and too changeable. For example, if someone says, "Bear left," would you move to the left or would you think there's a dangerous bear in the woods to your left? Or, if you were told to "read the charges," would you be reading a list of what you bought in a store or a criminal charge in court? See what I mean?

A computer doesn't think for itself. It also doesn't have the common sense that would allow it to choose between two meanings for the same word. Because of this, all computer languages are very precise. They have exact rules for how you write a command and how to use symbols, and strictly controlled vocabularies. If an unknown word is introduced into the language, it must be clearly defined before it can be used.

Biologist Miriam Barlow and mathematician Kristina Crona are writing a computer program called Time Machine. Focusing on the gene that makes a bacteria resistant to antibiotics, the program then decides which antibiotics should be given in which order to avoid resistance. Using their Time Machine program, Barlow and Crona have prevented and then reversed resistance in the lab. Antibiotic resistance is the number-one issue of modern medicine. Around two million people are infected and twenty-three thousand die from antibiotic resistant bacteria each year.

Since a computer is a mechanical thing, it needs to be talked to in a way that it will understand. Chris Kite from Codeconquest.com explained it like this:

A computer can only understand two distinct types of data: on and off. In fact, a computer is really just a collection of on/off switches (transistors). Anything that a computer can do is nothing more than a unique combination of some transistors turned on and some transistors turned off.

Binary code is the representation of these combinations as 1s and 0s, where each digit represents one transistor. Binary code is grouped into bytes, groups of 8 digits representing 8 transistors. For example, 11101001. Modern computers contain millions or even billions of transistors, which means an unimaginably large number of combinations.

But one problem arises here. To be able to write a computer program by typing out billions of 1s and 0s would require superhuman brainpower, and even then it would probably take you a lifetime or two to write. This is where programming languages come in.[1]

English, the Language of Languages

Throughout the history of computer languages, the trend has been to write keywords and code libraries in English. All of the most common computer languages are examples of this.

Why? Because English was the language of those who wrote the first computer languages and many of those that were written afterward. Thousands of computer languages were developed in the United States, hundreds in England, and a couple hundred in Canada and Australia, all English-speaking countries.

In countries where English is not the native language, programmers still write their languages in English in an effort to gain international appeal. For example, Python is in English, but it was developed in the Netherlands. The same is true for Ruby, which was developed in Japan.

Here are a few interesting languages that are not written in English.

⇨ AMMORIA, written in Arabic

⇨ 丙正正, the Chinese version of C++

⇨ ドリトル or Dolittle, written in Japanese

⇨ Hanbe, written in Korean

⇨ Robik, written in Russian to teach coding to kids

In order for the computer to understand any language, it has to be translated. This happens when the programmer writes the source code and sends it through a compiler. Compiling software is specifically written to translate source code into assembly language and then translate the assembly language into machine code or binary code that the computer understands. This process is called compiling, and each language has its own compiler.

There are thousands of computer languages. But don't let that scare you. Most programmers work with only one or two. Take a look at the following list. It will help you decide which language fits that area of computer programming that interests you.

Types of Computer Languages

<Low-Level Languages/>

Low-level languages are used to write code that the computer understands without any help. These languages are linked to specific types of computers.

⇨ **Machine language** is code written using a string of zeros (0) and ones (1). A computer can easily understand instructions that are written this way, but it is difficult to write and varies from computer to computer, depending on the computer's processor. Machine language uses this binary number system where 0s and 1s represent "on–off," "open–close," or "go–no go." The command to add two numbers is written like this: 0110101100101000.

⇨ **Assembly language**, like ASM or Assembler, is one step above machine language. It uses short "reminder" code or chunks of code that hold specific instructions. The programmer can give the reminder code a name. The command to add two numbers is written like this: add pay, total.

Name: Haydn
Age: 13
Job (when not studying!): Software Program Writer

When did you first discover that you were interested in writing code?

I was ten. I was looking for interesting summer camps and found a class through the Saturday Academy. When I went to the class, it was a simple "point and click" type of learning, but it got me interested in programming. Shortly after this, I began using a game website called Roblox, which is a kids' programming engine where users can create their own games. I was interested at first, but I eventually became bored with the majority of the games. Because the website was designed for the creation of games, I realized that I wouldn't be bored if I could make games whenever I wanted. So, for Christmas, I asked for private coding lessons. I watched a multitude of online tutorials for programming on Roblox, and I also got some books about using Roblox for Christmas. My mom found a teacher (Edwin) and he worked with me over Skype. He would call me, and we would work together on a shared screen. I learned all about what you can do with programming, including how to debug code (figure out why it isn't working).

How did you learn to write code, and what languages do you know?

I learned to write in Lua, which is an open source language that is useful for storing data and gaming. Every programming engine that I use has a lot of extra tools that I can use tailored to what the engine is used for, besides the basic programming in every engine that uses Lua. By reading books, I learned some HTML, CSS, Java, and JavaScript. I also found out that once you understand your first language, the others are much easier to learn.

One program I wrote helped me with math problems. I was tired of the repetition of my math homework, so I wrote a program that solved them for me. I told my teacher what I'd done. He asked how using a program would help me remember the formulas for the test. I said that if I knew them well enough to write the code, then I'd know them when it came time to take the test. Also, I see the formula every time I use the program, and that reinforces it in my mind.

Another program I created using Codea on my iPad was a program that allows me to draw pictures using straight lines. It was point-to-point drawing where I could choose two points and then a line would appear between them. In my second version, I added the touch-and-drag feature, which makes it easier to choose where you want the lines to end. I also created my own tic-tac-toe game.

You participated in Hour of Code at school. What did you learn during that class?

The Hour of Code at my school focused on learning with games and trying to teach us coding concepts like loops and steps. It wasn't actual coding. If I were teaching the class, I'd show kids how to make something appear on the screen, how to play with it, and then how to change it using a real programming language. That way, kids won't be bored and can be creative; they can see coding in action, instead of it being just a theory.

Since you've tried learning to write code several different ways (classes, tutor, books), which way do you prefer?

I like to learn in all three ways. The classes give me a great understanding of coding concepts, and the teacher is there to answer questions. The tutoring was great because I got to work on what was interesting to me. I could ask questions and have them answered right away. Learning from a book takes longer because I have to interpret what the writer is trying to say and interpret the code that's written on the page. If you don't have the engine for a language you are learning, it's hard not seeing what's happening with the code. I have to use online resources for that.

Why do you think it's important for your peers to learn to write code?

Computer science engineers are going to be in high demand. While some jobs may go away when programs make them automatic, the core software programmer will always be needed. This makes it a stable career too. As technology is increasingly present in our lives, the need for programmers will increase as well. Also, writing code forces you to learn how to look at a problem in different ways. Failure is part of the process, and you have to learn to not let it get you down.

Do you have any tips for beginning coders?

For practice, I like to look at programs and think about how they wrote them. Don't let a failed program get you down. Keep going and learn from your mistakes. Work hard and be a problem solver. And, if possible, have two monitors. It really helps to have the coding on one and the graphics on the other. It makes it easier to see what you are doing and the impact of each change you make.

Where do you see yourself in ten years?

My plan is to go to college and get a computer science degree. Then I'd like to get a good job and possibly go on for an advanced degree to allow for an evolving career.

```
0100100100100100100100100100100100100100010010
```

<High-Level Languages/>

High-level languages are further away from machine and assembly languages. Any code written using them must pass through a

compiler and be translated into machine language, so the computer can understand it. High-level languages are closer to human language and, thus, are easier to write and easier to read, and it's easier to detect errors in them. High-level languages fall into specific groups. Here are the groups and a few languages that fall under each one.

➪ **Algorithmic languages** use a set of very specific instructions, written in a specific order, to achieve a specific goal. The programmer can write subprograms that can be reused. Each set of instructions works with others to achieve a predictable end result. Some algorithmic languages include:

- Fortran: Designed in 1957 by John Backus and his team for IBM, it is used for scientific applications.
- LISP: Developed in the late 1950s by John McCarthy at MIT, it is used for artificial intelligence programming.
- C: Developed in 1972 by Dennis Ritchie and Ken Thompson for AT&T, it is used for writing the code for operating systems. C and its descendants, C++ (which is also object oriented) and C++++, are some of the most commonly used languages. C is used in 3-D programming, game programming, and mobile applications.

➪ **Business-oriented languages** are designed to manage the large amounts of data generated by businesses like banks and investment companies. Some business-oriented languages include:

- COBOL: Widely used in the 1960s and 1970s, it was intended to be used for keeping records. Programs written in COBOL accounted for most of the problems associated with Y2K (Year 2000), or the Millennium bug. The language called for the use of two digits to represent a calendar year. For example, 72 in the date field meant "1972." Using two digits saved two bytes per record, times millions of records, which was a lot of storage savings back then. Because of this issue, when the new millennium came, much of the original code had to be rewritten.

- SQL: *SQL* stands for "structured query language" and is used to write programs that use databases. Databases are collections of bits of information. Using SQL, coders can query humongous databases to find chunks of specific information like "find every person with the last name of Smith" or "find females who own a cat."

⇨ **Education-oriented languages** were created for students and professors to use at universities. They tend to be easier to understand and perfect for beginning learners.

- BASIC: Designed in the mid-1960s by John Kemeny and Thomas Kurtz at Dartmouth College, it is easy to learn and intended for novice users. Its simple structure and small size made it popular when the personal computer arrived on the scene.
- Pascal: Designed in 1970 in Switzerland by Niklaus Wirth, its purpose was to teach programming to students. It was loaded on most computers in the 1970s and 1980s.

⇨ **Object-oriented languages** were created to help manage large programs. These languages have prepackaged code, called objects, which perform specific operations. Users are taught when and where to use each object, but they never see the code written inside. Complex objects can also be built by using a variety of objects and telling them to interact with each other.

- Java: Designed in the early 1990s by James Gosling for Sun Microsystems, Inc., it was intended for use in writing interactive programs for the world wide web (www). It is widely used to write programs for small, portable devices like mobile phones and is one of the most popular programming languages. The Java motto is "Write once, run anywhere."

- Visual Basic .NET: Microsoft developed this to expand on BASIC by including buttons, menus, and other graphical elements to make writing code more user-friendly.

 # \<Spotlight/\>

Augusta Ada Byron King, Countess of Lovelace (1815–1852), World's First Computer Programmer

Augusta Ada Byron was born in London, England, on December 10, 1815, to Lord George and Lady Anne Byron. Her father, a Romantic poet, separated from her mother when Ada was a month old. Three months later, he left England and never returned. Byron never met her famous father, who died when she was eight.

Her mother, a well educated and very religious woman, tried to suppress Byron's poetic tendencies by requiring that she be tutored in mathematics and logic. It was that training, along with her natural artistic abilities, that helped her design a flying machine when she was only thirteen years old.

When she was seventeen, Byron met a man who would help define her life and career. She was introduced to Charles Babbage, a mathematician, inventor, and mechanical engineer, who would become known as the father of the computer. She was in constant communication with him, and he mentored her on almost every subject. Babbage gave her the affectionate nickname "Enchantress of Numbers."

In 1835, at the age of twenty, Byron married Baron William King and became a baroness. When her husband inherited the title of Earl of Lovelace in 1838, she gained the title of Countess Lovelace. The couple had three children.

When Charles Babbage lost his government funding, the countess became his defender and a wealthy supporter of his work. For nine months, she worked on translating Italian mathematician Luigi Menabrea's book about Babbage's Analytical Engine, *Notions sur la machine analytique de Charles Babbage*. When she was finished with the translation, she added her own notes, which explained how the machine functioned and how it differed from the difference engine.

Deep in Countess Lovelace's notes for the book, in Section G, she wrote detailed instructions on how to use Babbage's Analytical Engine to calculate a sequence of Bernoulli numbers. Her calculations would have run correctly if the engine had been built, but it never was. However, her instructions are considered the first computer program and she is considered the first computer programmer.

In the late 1970s, the US Department of Defense honored her by naming their high-level programming language Ada. Ada is still in use today.

⇨ **Declarative languages** are very high-level languages. Programs written in these languages focus on what the programmer wants done rather than how to do it. They fall into two categories, logic languages and functional languages.
- PROLOG: This is a logic language used for artificial intelligence projects.
- HOPE and REX: These functional languages are used as research tools in academia.

⇨ **Document-formatting languages** were developed to help organize text and graphics on the printed page. They are used to write code that defines parts of a document like paragraphs, indents, fonts, and margins; performs the tasks of a word processor; and talks to a printer.

- TeX: Developed between 1977 and 1986 by Donald Knuth at Stanford University, this language gives control over all the things associated with a professional-looking document, including the inclusion of tables and graphics.
- PostScript: Developed in the 1980s by Adobe Systems, this language is used to describe a document so it can be displayed on a computer screen or interpreted by a printer. It is free for anyone to use and works well with high-resolution laser printers.

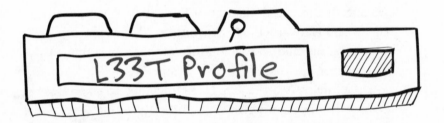

Name: Zach Galant
Job: Cofounder, CodeHS

When did you first become interested in writing computer code and decide to make it the focus of your career?
In middle school, I wanted to make my own video games. I enjoyed playing video games, but even more, I wanted to change how they worked and make them my own way. Throughout the rest of middle and high school, I learned as much as I could about creating games and websites. It wasn't until I got to college that I did any "real programming." Everything I had done before used some sort of drag-and-drop system that wasn't really using a professional programming language. My first quarter at Stanford, I took the introductory programming class that taught Java, and I was hooked. I had learned many of the concepts through game

creation, so everything in Java made sense to me. I spent all of my Thanksgiving and winter breaks coding and knew then that it was what I wanted to do.

What education/work path did you take to get where you are today?

My high school didn't offer any programming classes, so I was self-taught until college. In college, I majored in computer science. During my summers, I focused on using the skills I learned in classes out in the real world to reinforce and improve upon what I learned. I had an internship one summer making iPad apps, and another summer I worked on a start-up project with a few friends. Then, during spring quarter my senior year, I started CodeHS and have been learning even more since then.

Describe the kind of programming work you do.

I have done several different kinds of programming work, including game design, iPhone app creation, web development, and artificial intelligence. At CodeHS, my main focus is on web development. This means that I'm writing the code that builds the website you use when you're learning on CodeHS.

You are the founder of Tera Byte Video Game Creation Camp. What motivated you to start this camp?

When I was in the seventh grade, I went to a summer camp in Los Angeles where I learned to create video games. After I went home to Dallas, I kept learning more and more about it. The next summer, I realized that a similar camp did not exist in Dallas, so I decided to start my own. Since I had been practicing video game creation all year, I was confident that I would be able to teach beginners, so I jumped in and went for it.

You also have a website, CodeHS.com. Why did you decide to build this site, and what are your goals for it?

My cofounder, Jeremy Keeshin, and I both spent several years at Stanford helping teach programming classes. We were both section leaders and then head teaching assistants for the main introductory programming classes. During our senior year, we found that there were amazing opportunities in online education. Since access to quality computer science educational materials was not very widespread, we set out to build CodeHS to give anyone around the world access to the same quality programming education that students at Stanford could get.

What do you enjoy most and least about writing code?
The best part of writing code is that you are in control. The computer will do whatever you ask of it as long as you know how to ask. This is very empowering because you can create anything that interests you. What I enjoy least is getting stuck when using tools I've never used before, particularly when there is little documentation about how to use those tools. It can be frustrating if you don't have someone working with you to help talk through the problems.

What do you see in the future for computer programming and/or for programmers?
The future for programmers is very promising. There will be millions of available jobs for programmers in a wide range of industries. Coding isn't just for making games or websites. People who know coding will be writing code for movies, sports companies, fashion companies, entertainment, and more. Knowing how to code opens doors to many possibilities.

What advice would you give to a young person who is interested in becoming a programmer?
Keep practicing and don't give up. Coding can be difficult and frustrating sometimes, but it is also really rewarding once you figure it out. Don't get intimidated by people who know more than you do. Nobody was born knowing how to code. Anyone who knows more than you was at the place you are at some point, and if they figured it out, you can too!

```
010010010010010010010010010010010010010010
```

⇨ **Standard generalized markup languages** (SGML) are metalanguages, languages used to talk about code that is written in another computer language. SGML is recognized by every nation as a way of creating "tags" that specify the function of a piece of code or how it should be displayed. For example, depending on the language, a tag written like this <emphasis> could be defined as underlining the text, using italics, or changing the font to bold.

- DocBook: This is used for technical documentation.
- LinuxDoc: This is used for the Linux documentation project, an all-volunteer project that publishes documentation for Linux programs online for everyone to use.

⇨ **World Wide Web** display languages are used to create the pages you see on sites across the internet. Each page contains text, graphics, audio, and links to other pages.

- HTML: Designed by Tim Berners-Lee in the 1980s for the European Council for Nuclear Research (CERN) physics laboratory in Switzerland, it works using tags that specify elements on a web page, like tables, headers, columns, and font sizes. An HTML web page is sent through a web browser that interprets the tags and then displays the page for the viewer to see. HTML is also used for writing applications for mobile devices.
- XML: Created in response to the fact that HTML cannot be extended to add new text elements, XML makes it easy to explain where a command begins and ends. To indicate the start of an italicized phrase, you'd write this <ITAL>, and to indicate when to stop italicizing, you'd write </ITAL>. When programmers define new tags, XML allows them to write rules that the browser understands, so the page is displayed properly.

➡️ **Web-scripting languages** were developed to add reader interaction with web pages. Scripts are used when someone wants to fill in a form or order a product on a website. You can use any programming language to write scripts, but a simple text language like Perl works well. There are also languages designed specifically for writing script.

- JavaScript: Designed by Netscape Communications, it can be used with Netscape and Microsoft browsers.
- VB Script: This was developed by Microsoft for use with its Microsoft Office suite of programs.

G-code is a highly specialized machining language that is used in computer-aided manufacturing (CAD) to tell a tool how to make something. For example, it is used to write instructions that tell a cutting tool where to start, what path to take, and how fast to move as it cuts away material, leaving a finished piece behind. G-code is also used for processes that tell tools to form things (building up instead of taking away), like 3-D printers.

Choosing Your First Language

Choosing your first programming language can be hard. Which one you choose will depend on where your interests lie and what type of programs you want to write. Keeping the list above in mind and reading the information and interviews in this book will help you narrow down your choices.

Whatever language you choose, remember that learning the first one is the hardest. Once you understand the basics, learning each additional language gets easier. Having said that, here is some additional information that might help you make a choice.

1. **Python** is simple and easy to learn, and you can do a lot with it. It is used in many computer science introductory

classes in the United States. The code is easy to read, and you will learn good programming style. Python is fun to learn. And because it's fun, you will probably write successful programs, become confident, and continue to learn. Python is growing in popularity because it is used on Pinterest and Instagram.

2. **C** is the most widely used programming language. Like every doctor needs to know anatomy, every programmer should know C. By learning C, you will learn the fundamentals of programming at the lowest level, the hardware level. You will understand how computers work in a way that isn't possible if you only learn a higher-level language. This language is not beginner friendly.

3. **Java** is the second most popular programming language. It's been around for a long time, and once you've learned it, you can easily learn other languages. It's used for many purposes, including mobile app development, and can run on any operating system.

4. **JavaScript** is great if you want to jump in and build your own website. Web browsers already have the capability to understand it. It has easy rules, and you'll learn the basics of programming. And a big plus, you'll see immediate results from the code you write.

5. **PHP** has a large online community dedicated to helping new users. There are also a lot of books written about the language and a lot of classes available. You can also learn a lot from the large number of open source projects available online.

6. The **TIOBE Index** ranks programming languages according to their current popularity, not on whether or not you can find a job once you learn it. Their ranking of the top ten, from most to least popular: C, Java, Objective-C, C++, C#, PHP, JavaScript, Python, Visual Basic .NET, and Visual Basic.

Open Source Code

Open source code is code that is available for everyone to use. The idea is that many hands make light work. If many people are looking at the code, using the code, writing scripts for the code, and editing the code, it will become a bigger, better, and more powerful program.

Linux is the most popular open source computer operating system. The most popular open source software programs are WordPress, which is blogging software used on over 202 million websites; Magento, which is software used by over thirty million companies to sell products on the web; and Mozilla Firefox, which is a web browser used by over 24 percent of those who surf the web.

Quiz
Do You Speak My Language?

Computer languages allow a programmer to tell the computer what they want it to do. High-level languages resemble human speech, whereas low-level languages are much closer to the binary language that machines can understand. In this activity, you have examples of different lines of code in various languages. Your task is to decide which multiple choice option describes what the language is commanding.

1. In HTML, *<h3>Welcome Aboard</h3>* would create . . .

   A. *A medium-size header on a web page*

   B. *An image of a sailing ship*

   C. *A table with three columns*

2. In Ruby, *irb(main):005:0>* 3**2 means . . .

 A. *To calculate the difference between three and two*

 B. *To return to the third line and copy it twice*

 C. *To find the answer to three squared*

3. In JavaScript, the line *//We need to clean the previous 4 lines* will . . .

 A. *Do nothing. This is just a comment so you remember to fix a bug later.*

 B. *Ask a partner program to rework the previous four lines of code.*

 C. *Start an editor that will fix the previous four lines of code automatically.*

4. In JavaScript, *confirm("I can definitely learn to code!")* will . . .

 A. *Create an error and possibly crash your computer.*

 B. *Cause a menu to appear that the user will have to interact with before moving on.*

 C. *Call up a quick-reference tutorial about learning to code.*

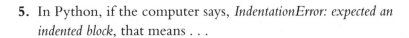

5. In Python, if the computer says, *IndentationError: expected an indented block*, that means . . .

 A. *There are too many spaces in the code you have just written*

 B. *There is not enough white space in the code you have just written.*

 C. *The code you have written is worthless and must be scrapped entirely.*

6. In Ruby, the method *"So, You Want to Write Computer Code?".reverse* will appear as . . .

   A. *"?edoC retupmoC etirW ot tnaW uoY ,oS"*

   B. *"Code? Computer Write to Want You So,"*

   C. *"Computer Code, You Want to write?"*

7. In HTML, *Coding is for everyone!* will produce text that is . . .

   A. *In bold font*

   B. *In large type*

   C. *All uppercase lettering*

8. In Python, the command *print "You're doing wonderfully!"* will . . .

   A. *Send the words* You're doing wonderfully! *to the nearest printer.*

   B. *Make the words* You're doing wonderfully! *appear on the computer's console.*

   C. *Add the title* You're doing wonderfully! *to a web page and make the lettering have a bold floral print.*

Writing Code

99 LITTLE BUGS IN THE CODE
1 BUG FIXED; WE COMPILE AGAIN
100 LITTLE BUGS IN THE CODE

When you are writing code, it helps to remember that there are many ways to get from an original idea to actual working code. Depending on the person, team, or company, the steps may change, but the general process remains the same.

For every program you write, you start by answering the question: What do I want this program to do? This takes time to nail down because you have to know exactly what you want. It's not okay to say, "I want a mouse to run across the screen." Instead, you need to be specific, "I want a red mouse to run from one corner of the screen to the other, along a cobblestone path." Once the code is written, you have to test it. Expect your first tests to fail. Each coder will get the mouse across the screen in a different way. That's the great thing about coding! There's no right or wrong way to get the mouse to its destination. If it arrives, you did it!

In the early days of writing software, coders borrowed the waterfall model from companies that manufactured products or constructed things like buildings or bridges. This process of writing software is still in use today and looks like this

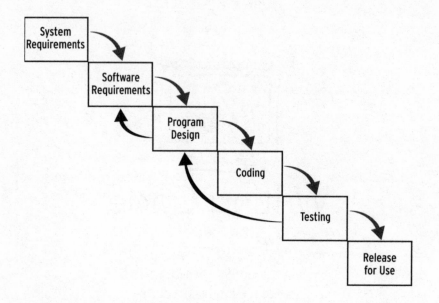

A newer method is called the test-driven development (TDD) cycle, and it looks like this:

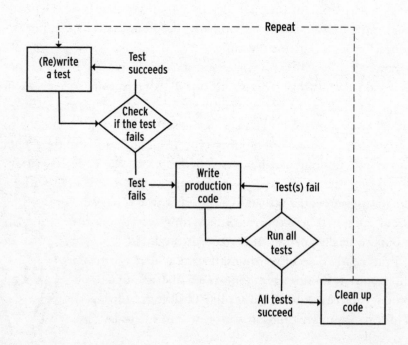

No matter which test cycle is used, every coder will spend a lot of time testing and retesting the code he or she writes. This process can't be skipped. So enjoy! Use it as a time to develop new ideas, solve old problems, and discover innovative ways to write complex code.

Concussions are a huge concern for those who play sports, are in the military, or work on dangerous construction sites. Coders working for X2biosystems have designed the xPatch that is placed behind a person's ear and monitors blows to the head. When a blow is detected, information is recorded and sent to an X2NET database. From there, all impacts are monitored and analyzed by trainers or doctors to help make decisions about the person's medical care and future brain health.

 # <Spotlight/>

Rear Admiral Grace "Amazing Grace" Hopper (1906–1992), Queen of Software

Grace Brewster Murray was born in New York City on December 9, 1906, the oldest of three children. She was a curious child, and at the age of seven, she took apart all the family's alarm clocks just to see how they worked.

At the age of seventeen, Murray went to Vassar, an all-women's college, and earned a bachelor's degree in mathematics and physics. From there, she went to Yale University, where she earned a master's degree and then a PhD in mathematics.

Hopper began her career teaching mathematics at Vassar and in 1941 was promoted to associate professor. Two years later, at the start of World War II, she took a leave of absence and joined the United States Navy Reserve. At the time, women weren't allowed in the military, so she joined the WAVES, Women Accepted for Volunteer Emergency Service. She trained at the Naval Reserve Midshipmen's School at Smith College and graduated first in her class.

In 1944, Hopper was assigned to the Bureau of Ships Computation Project at Harvard University, where she learned to program a Mark I computer. After the war, she remained in the Navy Reserve while also working as a research fellow at Harvard. One day, she was having trouble with the Mark II computer. It kept shorting out. She found a two-inch-long moth in the machine and told everyone that she had "debugged" the computer. The term stuck, and today it is still used by programmers to refer to fixing errors in their code.

After Harvard, Hopper took the position of senior mathematician with Ecker-Mauchly Computer Corporation. She worked on the team that developed the UNIVAC I (UNIVersal Automatic Computer I), which was the second commercial computer produced in the United States. She also studied various ways to turn mathematic code into a computer language. Her first working compiler was finished in 1952. "Nobody believed that I had a running compiler," she said. "Nobody would touch it. They told me computers could only do arithmetic."[1]

Despite those early doubters, by 1954, her company was releasing the first compiler-based programming languages under the names MATH-MATIC and FLOW-MATIC. These languages paved the way for a later computer compiling language known as COBOL (common business-oriented language), which is still in use today.

Hopper thought it was important that there be standards for testing computers and the software that runs on them. Thanks to her, today computing standards are set by the National Institute of Standards and Technology.

In 1966, she retired from the Navy Reserve with the rank of commander. She was recalled in 1967 and served for another ten years as director of the Navy Programming Languages Group during which she was promoted to captain.

In 1983, she was promoted again, this time by special presidential appointment, to the rank of rear admiral lower half. She retired again in 1986, becoming the oldest serving officer in the US Navy. She died in 1992 at the age of eighty-five and was buried with full military honors in Arlington National Cemetery in Washington, DC. The Naval destroyer, USS *Hopper*, launched in 1996 and bears her name.

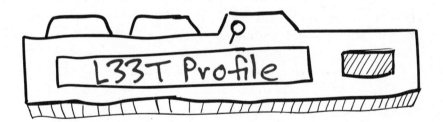

Name: Tesca Fitzgerald
Job: Computer science PhD student and graduate research assistant, Georgia Institute of Technology

When did you first become interested in writing computer code and decide to make it the focus of your career?
I started working on computers at a very early age. My parents had computers around the house, so I became familiar with playing games and typing on my parents' laptop.

When I was five, my sister joined a LEGO robotics club at our community center. When I decided to join, the coach took me aside and asked if I wanted to learn to program the robot. She taught me how to use the visual programming system, which let me program the robot by dragging action commands into sequence on the screen. I was very excited to see that by dragging and dropping action blocks on the screen, I could get the robot to move around, turn in a circle, or make a sound.

The other members of the team wanted to learn how to build the robot, but nobody else was interested in learning to program it. This gave me the chance to be the lead programmer of my team, starting in my first year, and it was a role I continued to play for the next seven years.

After several years of experience with programming, I started to look for a new challenge. I was already very familiar with the drag-and-drop interface of the programming system, so I worked on a project that would let me write out the robot's instructions in text, which would then be read and interpreted by a program built using the drag-and-drop interface. This required less time to program and would require less storage space on the robot, letting us store more programs on the robot. The process of working on this self-guided project and going beyond the typical programming system used for this robot was very exciting. It was during this project that I started to think of coding as a potential career.

What education/work path did you take to get to your current position?

My current work in graduate school involves academic research, which is all about working to solve problems that aren't answered in any textbook or website. I first became interested in research while working on science fair projects starting in middle school. Science fair projects are a great example of self-guided projects, where you, as the participant, get to define the topic of your own work and see it through to completion.

I became interested in artificial intelligence (AI) research while working on a science fair project to allow a LEGO robot to navigate between two points on its own. I realized that the task of getting from one point to another is simple enough for people to do every day without thinking, but it is actually very difficult for robots to do. Think about what steps you take to plan a route from where you are to your school or home. What information do you need in order to plan a good route? For a robot with less knowledge about navigation strategies and the obstacles that are in its way, route planning is quite a challenge. In trying to get a robot to address everyday problems that people solve easily, I realized just how complex human intelligence is. I continue to appreciate this even more as I work on AI research as a graduate student.

I worked on two additional research projects while completing my computer science degree in college. One of these projects was an honors thesis project, which is a self-guided project that a student completes with guidance from a professor. My honors thesis project was about programming a tool to help website designers test the interface of their website. The second project I worked on was a tool to help a current graduate student test his project. Working on this project as an assistant to a graduate student gave me an idea of what it might be like for me to be in a PhD program. During that same year, I applied to several computer science PhD programs around the country to work in artificial intelligence and robotics.

Explain your graduate work in cognitive science and robotics.

Cognitive science is about understanding how the human mind works to help us think, learn, remember, and reason. Since I started working on AI science fair projects, I became very interested in reflecting on human cognition to inspire new approaches to AI problems. Applying AI to robotics adds even more challenges, since robots that move around in the real world have to make sense of what they perceive and have to plan actions to let them interact with people and objects around them.

As we develop robots to be smarter, we expect them to be able to perform more humanlike tasks. However, many tasks that we encounter on a daily basis are difficult to do without experience and knowledge that we build up over time. As an example, making breakfast in the morning doesn't seem hard to do until you try to get a robot to do the same thing. This kind of problem, while difficult, excites me because it helps me appreciate how well people are able to solve problems, while also giving me the opportunity to solve new and interesting problems.

My graduate work is focused on getting robots to imitate tasks they see people do. Imitation is a skill that we use all the time; if you are learning to play a new sport or play a game for the first time, someone might teach you how to do it by showing you, rather than giving you a list of instructions. Robots don't have the same imitation ability, but this is a problem that many researchers are currently addressing. My graduate work is also addressing this problem. If we can get robots to learn in a way that is similar to how people learn, then they can learn more naturally and quickly than if we had to program the robot for each task.

What do you see in the future for robotics?
Robotics is such an interesting field because it makes us look at tasks that are easy for a person but much more difficult for a robot to attempt. Even simple actions like walking or climbing a ladder are very difficult for a robot, so there is no shortage of interesting and challenging robotics problems to be solved. I think that the future of robotics will involve robots that interact more with people, making them more common in helping out around the house, rescuing the injured in emergency situations that are too dangerous for human rescuers, or working alongside nurses in hospitals to take care of patients.

What tips do you have for kids interested in writing computer code?
Work on a project that you are personally interested in. There are lots of books and tutorials that can teach you how to write code for a generic project, but I find it to be much easier to learn something new when working on a project that I am excited about. One way to choose a project is to think about

the things you do in everyday life and how coding can help you with those tasks, such as a program to help you study for quizzes or an app that shows you a guidebook for taking care of a pet. Another way to find an interesting project is to think about the games you enjoy and how you might write the code for a game of your own. Once you find a project that you're personally interested in, learning how to write code for that project becomes more fun.

0100100100100100100100100100100100100010

Source Code and Object Code

Source code is the lines of text that make up every program. It is written in programming language and can be a few lines or millions of lines. Source code includes all the instructions that make a program function. It also includes comments from the programmer that state what he or she did and why. Short programs, called scripts, run directly from the source code.

Large programs require compiling. Compiling happens when code, written in any computer language, is run through a compiler. The compiler translates the code into language that the computer can understand: object code.

Teamwork

Most large computer programs take a team to create. From the original idea to the final product, programmers work together on each step to make sure the final product does what it's supposed to do and is free of bugs. Here's what a team might look like (titles may change from company to company):

Systems Architect or Systems Designer: Define the scope of the project for the Software Development Team. Communicate with a product manager, who is the one who works with the customer. Balance coder needs and customer wants.

Software Development Team: Take the system architect and system designer's vision and break the project into manageable pieces or sections. Assign each section to a team.

Section Programmer Team: Focus on their section of the program. Break the work into manageable parts.

Individual Programmers: Focus on writing their parts of the code.

Throughout the process of writing a piece of software, each level of the team is constantly communicating with the level above to make sure that the work is getting done properly and on time.

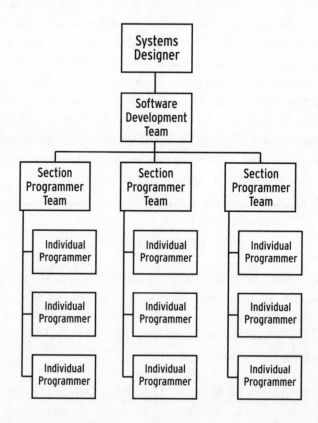

Validation and Verification (V&V)

Once a project is in place and the work has begun, each team sets a V&V process in place. This is how each team leader figures out if his or her team is staying on track.

Validation asks the question, "Are we building the right program?" It requires that the leader go back and make sure that the software is meeting the systems architect's and systems designer's needs.

Verification asks the question, "Are we building the program correctly?" It requires that each programmer make sure they are writing code that meets the specifications of the software development team.

There are international standards for how companies set up their software V&V processes. The standard for software development can be found in the Institute of Electrical and Electronics Engineers (IEEE) standard 1012-2012. The 1012-2012 standard is used by corporations around the world and is required by some companies, especially those working in high-risk areas, like nuclear power plants and the medical industry.

Source code editors are the number-one tool of every programmer. This software is designed to edit source code and can be a standalone application, built into a web browser, or part of a development package. It is used to help programmers edit their code as they write, find bugs in their code, and test their code.

Qualities of Good Code

⇨ It runs flawlessly and has no bugs.

⇨ It's readable, even by inexperienced programmers.

⇨ It's short and to the point. Programmers call this DRY, for Don't Repeat Yourself.

⇨ It works fast without hogging memory.

⇨ It's well written, even in areas where no one is supposed to see it.

⇨ It's organized—definitions of functions are not scattered throughout the software.

⇨ It documents all usage requirements.

⇨ It's reusable.

The computer mouse was invented by Douglas Engelbart and Bill English in the 1960s at the Stanford University Research Institute and was patented in 1970. The mouse was originally called an X-Y Position Indicator for a Display System. When asked how the mouse got its less convoluted—and downright cuter—name, Engelbart said, "No one can remember. It just looked like a mouse with a tail, and we all called it that."[2]

Best Ways to Learn a Language

⇨ Use an online training site like Code Academy or CodeHS. There are tons of them online, and many are free.

⇨ Play coding games that teach you the basic skills. There are many computer games and board games available.

⇨ Sign up for a coding course. If you're old enough, find a class at your high school, community college, local coding club, or college. If you are too young for those, ask your parents to find you a kids' programming class online.

⇨ Read coding books. There are lots of books written about every computer language. Some are free, some are eBooks, and some are traditional books you find at your local bookstore. Remember, some books can be poorly written or overly hard to understand. Don't stop at the first book on the subject matter, and get recommendations from others.

⇨ Find a mentor. Having someone to help you through the process is invaluable. They can get you over the bumps, keep you on track, and keep you moving forward.

⇨ Study other programmers' code. For some people, the best way to learn is to tear apart another programmer's work and see how that person did it. Don't be afraid—dissect away!

Name: Ethan Eirinberg
Age: 17
Job (when not studying!): Founder, CreateHS

When did you first discover that you were interested in writing code?
Ever since I was about six years old, I have had an interest in computers. When the app store for the iPhone came out, my older brother decided that he wanted to make an app. After a

year of learning, he put out his first app. I saw what he was able to produce, and it served as my inspiration to learn to code. In eighth grade, I really developed a passion for it.

How did you learn to write code, and what language(s) do you know?
In eighth grade, I pushed myself to learn how to code. To me, reading books on algorithms and theories behind languages is boring and unhelpful. I tried to avoid this way of learning by watching YouTube videos and constantly creating small projects.

As I entered high school, I was excited to learn in a more formal environment. Unfortunately, my school didn't teach computer science for freshmen or sophomores. I went back online, studied from Team Treehouse (an online tutorial site), and constantly pushed myself to keep creating new projects.

I believe that the best way to learn is to do. I have created many side projects and continue to do so to refine my skills. I currently know HTML, CSS, JavaScript, Java, Python, Flask, and I'm learning Swift.

Explain CreateHS, the coding competition you started.
When I realized that the best way to learn how to code was to keep putting out projects, I was determined to find a contest or competition to keep me motivated. After looking all over the internet, I could not find any project-based competitions for high school students.

I took what little web development skills I had and built a website called CreateHS. CreateHS was a recurring monthly competition where I posted an assignment and collected entries from kids around the world.

I recruited notable stars in the tech industry to serve as judges. Donations from top tech companies were given away as prizes. Judges included a billionaire, founders of popular programming languages, and CEOs of major corporations. Sponsors included Dropbox, Microsoft, GitHub, and Team Treehouse. More than anything, CreateHS gave me a chance to connect with kids just like me all across the world.

After about a year of monthly challenges, it became too difficult to find new judges and sponsors each month. I put it on hold, and I'm actively trying to figure out a way to scale it.

Why you think it's important that your peers learn how to write code?
Because it teaches you to think differently. Regardless of whether or not you go into a career in computer science, knowledge of computers will ultimately end up having an effect on your career. In the end, who doesn't want the ability to create whatever you dream up in your head?

How do you balance your schoolwork with all your other activities?
I prioritize schoolwork above anything else. I'm driven to get into one of the top computer science schools in the country. Not solely because they would offer the best computer science education but because of the other students I hope to be surrounded by.

Where do you see yourself in ten years?
I hope to own a tech company in Silicon Valley. I'm not sure what its purpose will be, but I know that I want to go to the Bay Area and work in tech.

`0100100100100100100100100100100100100010`

The Process Continues

Even after a piece of software is written, there is more work to be done. Coders work to keep existing software current. They write upgrades. They fix errors that crop up after customers start using the software, and they add new functions that their customers request.
    The final duty of a coder is to decide how and when a piece of hardware or software becomes obsolete. This can be a difficult

decision, since hundreds of programmer-years could have gone into the original application. This process is called sunsetting, intentionally phasing out or terminating the use of a program. Sunsetting is sometimes decided at the time the software is written, but more often it happens when a program takes more work to maintain than it's worth. This step is very important because it ensures the following:

⇨ Sensitive information is not revealed.

⇨ There is a smooth transition to a new system or software program.

⇨ Information is properly archived.

⇨ Information is properly destroyed.

In an attempt to get kids excited about coding, Google has introduced the Blockly project. It is a way for kids to write computer programs without typing on a keyboard. Blockly Games use blocks that look like puzzle pieces that snap together to create a program. Each game builds on the next and easily introduces kids to increasingly difficult programming tasks. After mastering games like Maze, Bird, Turtle, Movie, and Pond, the student is switched to regular text-based programming. Blockly is available to kids around the world and is translated in many languages, including Klingon!

The Future of Coding

⇨ There will be a need for speed! GPUs are in, CPUs are out. Central processing units in the computer are being replaced by graphics processing units.

⇨ As the need for speed increases because of the massive amounts of data that need to be processed, coders are looking for new and innovative ways to break down their programs into manageable pieces. They'll continue the work on the difficult problem of simultaneous computations through the use of symmetrical multiprocessing (SMP) and multithreading (MT).

⇨ It's all about Big Data. Databases will rule the world. More and more information is being stored on bigger and bigger databases. The future is in how best to manipulate the data and how fast it can be done.

⇨ JavaScript will rule! Peter Wyner from InfoWorld said, "The mainframe will have Cobol. Biologists will probably stick with Python. Linux will be written in C. But almost everything else is fair game as JavaScript gobbles the world."[3]

⇨ It'll be Android for everyone! The Android operating system is swallowing up the competition.

⇨ Programmers will be in demand. Even with the introduction of programming to more and more younger kids, only certain brains grasp the mathematical, logical, complex world of writing code. If yours is one of those, jump on the train and enjoy the ride.

Quiz
Destination: Unknown

Computer coders are really good at taking a big problem and breaking it down into smaller steps. Once they understand the steps, they write an algorithm, or list of instructions, that tells the computer what to do. In this activity, you and a friend will practice communicating steps clearly, the way a coder must clearly and logically communicate algorithms to the computer.

You will need:

Sheets of grid paper
Two pencils

Instructions:

Setup

1. Decide which player will be the Computer, and which will be the Coder.
2. Give one sheet of grid paper to the Computer. This is the memory map.
3. Give the other sheet of grid paper to the Coder. This is the program.
4. Choose one square along either edge of the grid paper as the start box. Mark it with an *s*. The papers should look identical when done.

Game Play

1. Computer: Choose one square on the map to be the destination square and mark it with an *X*. *Don't let the Coder see your mark.* Your destination square must be in the farthest quadrant from the start square. This means if the start square is on the top right side of the page, your destination square must be on the left and lower half of the page.
2. Coder: Your job is to find the Computer's destination square. Give instructions for where the Computer should move (beginning at the square labeled with an *s*). Be specific: "Move forward one square" or "Move left three squares" are good instructions. "Go one square" is not a good instruction because it doesn't give the Computer a direction in which to move.
3. Using pencils, both players draw a line from box to box, following the Coder's instructions, until

the Computer reaches the destination point. The Computer cannot speak, only follow the Coder's instructions.

4. Coder: When the Coder finds the destination square, the Computer should say, "Application complete."
5. Next count how many moves it took for the Coder to get the Computer to the destination square.
6. Switch places and repeat the game. Whichever Coder gets their Computer to the destination square in the fewest moves is the winner.

Mix It Up

1. The Computer can add black dots to several of the squares. These will be glitches. If the Coder directs the Computer over one of these glitches, he or she must add two moves to their total score.
2. The Computer can mark boxes on the grid with smiley faces. The Coder must pass over at least one smiley face before reaching the destination point.
3. The Coder can try to combine instructions so that the Computer can move more quickly along a path. For example, the Coder can say, "Move forward one space and left three spaces." This gives precise instructions and helps the game go faster.
4. A bigger grid can add interest.

Reflection

⇨ How does this activity relate to writing code?

⇨ Would finding the destination square be easier if the Coder could see it? How might this relate to a real-world coder's need to think through problems and have a specific goal in mind?

⇨ Did having to pass over the smiley faces make the game harder? If so, why?

⇨ Was there ever a time when the Computer couldn't move due to unclear commands? What did the Coder have to do to make the commands clearer?

⇨ How does the size of the grid change the way the Coder states commands? Would the process be any different if the grid was larger? Smaller?

Systems and Application Coders

Question: How many programmers does
it take to change a lightbulb?

ANSWER: NONE. THAT'S A HARDWARE PROBLEM.

The first computers were huge! They were so large that they filled entire rooms. For decades, they were used only by scientists and engineers who worked for large corporations or universities. Those who programmed these computers focused on making them do specific tasks. The work was time-consuming and very precise.

When the vacuum tube was replaced by transistors in the mid-1950s, computers became smaller. They used less electricity, emitted less heat, and could handle a lot more data. Within another decade, transistors were replaced by integrated circuits, and the use of computers for commercial and personal use exploded.

Next came the invention of the microprocessor, which allowed computers to become even smaller and led to the next boom in computer sales and the introduction of the personal computer or PC. With the arrival of the PC came the desire for mobility. This is a movement that continues to today as people demand more and more functionality in smaller and smaller devices.

Coders at Open Bionics, a British start-up company, are designing a program that creates hands using a 3-D printer! Their hands are expected to cost about one-tenth of what other prosthetic hands on the market cost. If testing goes as planned, Open Bionics hopes to release the product under a noncommercial license in 2016. A noncommercial license allows charities and amputees to use the designs but not for-profit companies. Their company slogan? "We're arming the masses!"

You are living in the computer age. Almost everything you hear, everything you see, and everything you do is connected, in some way, to a computer. Your television streams video, you read books and magazines on an eReader, you play games on a myriad of devices, and your first job will probably require that you know how to use a computer. All of that technology would not exist without computer coders who write the code that keeps these devices functioning.

Name: Emory Penney
Job: Software engineer, Intel Corporation

When did you first become interested in writing computer code and decide to make it the focus of your career?
I was always good with computers. Starting when I was about ten years old, my friends and older family members would have

me fix their computers. I didn't really spend any time thinking about programming until my junior year of high school. Frankly, I was looking for an easy elective credit, and my school offered an intro to computer programming course. I thought, since math and computers came easily to me, it would be an easy A. I was surprised by how challenging the class was. I was barely treading water the first six weeks. Then one day, it just clicked for me. It was the first time in my life I found something that was both challenging and fun.

What education/work path did you take to get to your current position?

After I took that programming class, I started applying for high school internships with Intel. I interviewed for several and discovered I had a lot to learn. I spent much of my summer in front of my computers learning to program, writing silly little apps just to sharpen my skills. I wrote a web tool where you input two dates, and it computes how much time there was between those dates (sort of a countdown timer). I remember I got hung up for weeks trying to get all the leap-year rules programmed correctly. I also wrote a tool that retrieved all the artist and album information and embedded it into the metadata of my music collection.

Early in the fall of my senior year, I was accepted for an internship in Intel's software division. I spent a year soaking up every bit of knowledge I could from those guys before I went off to college. I didn't finish college because of the overwhelming costs. But after I left school, I worked at a series of temporary jobs at Intel and other local companies; each position was nine to twelve months, and I worked on a variety of different projects. It was hard work and long hours. I learned everything I could from every experience. Gradually, I established a reputation as a hard worker and strong problem solver. My reputation and skills eventually led to a full-time job at Intel, doing what I love!

Describe your past job as a build and release engineer.

I'm having a hard time answering this one in simple English—for the seven years I was with this team, one of our longest-running jokes was how hard it was to describe what we did . . .

The organization I worked for was responsible for bringing order to the chaos that is software development. One of our primary missions was creating accountability between the developer who checked in the code, the stakeholder who asked for the change, and the actual bits that were shipped to a customer. We created abstract relationships between bugs, their submitters, the fixes for those bugs, and the individual nightly releases that were impacted by those bugs. We supported nearly a dozen software development teams here in the Hillsboro and in Santa Clara, California, as well as multiple places in Israel and Germany.

Our goal was to enable someone five years from now to be able to easily determine: Why was this change submitted? Who submitted it? When did they submit it? What release(s) of the software did and did not contain that change? And what did the source code look like at that time?

It's a lot of data to keep straight, especially when you're processing as many as fifteen thousand builds a month, most of which never see the light of day but still have to be accounted for. In many ways, the position was a cross between librarian and accountant. Not only did we have to inventory the contents of the releases but we also had to manage the archival of the old releases. The automation challenges involved were extraordinarily challenging but fun!

Describe your current position as a validation lead.

In my role as validation lead, I'm responsible for the quality of our product releases. I work with developers and management to understand any changes that are coming into the product and design and plan for how we're going to verify those changes and maintain product quality. Are there security implications to this new feature? Is our product using a new platform (Windows 10, Android Marshmallow, etc.)? Once I've assessed the impacts, I take action to change our test process.

I wear a few hats, including lab manager, automation developer, and team lead.

My role as lab manager requires me to keep a pool of computers, tablets, and phones running and useful to our developers. As team lead, I spend a lot of time in meetings and working with our sibling teams and organizations here and in Russia to provide input on delivery schedules and updates on product quality. As automation developer, I write scripts that test our functionality, design automation that integrates our tests with the build and release process, and also maintain infrastructure that monitors the up status of our servers and test systems.

Describe the process your team goes through to write a validation program.

We identify what needs to be validated; usually this is a new feature or some enhancement. We sit down and discuss how this new feature is supposed to behave: What does it do? How is the customer going to use it? What can they do with it? What should they not be able to do with it? And how do we break it?

Once we've answered these questions, we can write a test plan. The first iteration of this is usually a list of manual steps a human can take to validate that a new feature is behaving as expected. After we've written the manual steps, it's a matter of writing software that impersonates the humans: execute the steps outlined in the test plan and check the behavior and notify us if at any point in the process the software gives us unexpected output.

Of course, validation software (like any software) is subject to its own bugs. So at the end of the day, we need to have humans verifying the software too. Otherwise, we would have to write automation to test our automation and so on; then who watches the watcher?

What does an average workday look like for you?

Most mornings I sit down at my computer between 8:00 and 9:00, depending on if I'm actively collaborating with people overseas. I've had times where I start phone meetings as early as 7:00. The first thing I do is check my email. While I've been sleeping, people on the other side of the world have been working and are just finishing up their day. I follow up on any questions and problems that may have come up overnight.

Next, I run down a checklist of production systems I own. I verify that everything is still online and running as expected, and I follow up on our overnight tests and any other scheduled automation. We have a daily sync with everyone in my team, every day at around 10:00. This meeting is a place for everyone to report on what they got done and what they are working on, as well as ask the team for help solving problems they cannot solve by themselves.

Depending on the day, the rest of my routine consists of a mix of meetings, writing documentation, writing/updating automation, configuring test hardware (Android tablets, Windows virtual machines). Every day is different, with a different set of goals.

What do you see in the future for computer coding careers?

There is no shortage of software that needs to be written, and as technology becomes more complex and more entwined with our world, there are increasingly complex and interesting problems to solve. I think anyone with an interest and passion for solving these problems should just go for it! Even if it turns out to not be for you, hopefully, you'll walk away with a better understanding and appreciation for how all the gadgets in your life work.

Do you have any tips for kids who are interested in becoming coders?

The internet makes it so easy to teach yourself how to program. There are millions of online programming tutorials that are really great. I would encourage you to focus first on doing things that you find fun. There's no reason your first project needs to be revolutionary or innovative, as long as it's interesting to you. I would also suggest finding a few like-minded kids to work with. You don't necessarily need to collaborate on projects, but it's nice to have someone to look over your code when you get stuck.

0100100100100100100100100100100100010010010

Job Titles for Coders

Looking at all the job titles for people who write code could send you to the funny farm! There are many out there, and by the time you are ready to work in the industry, there may be many more. Trust me, once you are in the industry, the subtle differences in terminology will become crystal clear.

For now, here are a few key titles that cover most of the code-writing industry. These titles are often prefaced by the main program language that a person knows, like C++, Java, or Fortran. There are also job titles with prefaces like "web" and "cloud."

⇨ Developer

⇨ Programmer

⇨ Software Engineer

It is important to note that anyone who works in this industry has skills that go beyond his or her ability to write computer code. As a coder, you will write, debug, and maintain the detailed instructions that computers need to perform their tasks. Beyond that, you will need strong communication skills, project management skills, the ability to listen and understand user needs, as well as the ability to work on a team and manage your time.

Skills Coders Use Each Day

⇨ Write code using a number of different languages.

⇨ Write test programs and scripts to test programs.

⇨ Update existing programs so they work faster.

⇨ Write code that expands on the functions of a program, like adding the ability to print.

⇨ Work with a team to design a map of a new computer system or a new application.

⇨ Test for bugs in a program and correct the errors. This is called debugging.

⇨ Find pieces of regularly used code and create a snippet, a small chunk of reusable code. Snippets help speed up the coding process.

⇨ Insert comments into projects so coworkers can follow your process.

⇨ Work with developers, engineers, and application architects to keep projects going in the right direction.

There are many different types of coders, and finding the area that's right for you can be challenging. This isn't an exhaustive list, but here are the main areas where computer coders focus their work. Hopefully, one of them will pique your interest and you'll be inspired to learn more.

Systems Programmers

Systems programmers write operating systems, the code that is the brain of every computer.

Where Coders Work

⇨ Corporate information technology departments (IT)

⇨ Large software companies like Microsoft, Oracle, Amazon, and Dell

⇨ Small service firms that focus on web design, games, and business applications

⇨ Consulting companies as contract workers for various clients

⇨ Organizations like hospitals, schools and universities, insurance companies, airports, retail stores, manufacturing firms, and the government

⇨ Anywhere that produces a product containing a microprocessor

<Computer Systems Architects or Designers/>

Computer systems architects and designers work closely with customers to figure out what they need to run their companies. They focus on entire networks of computer systems and applications to make sure that they all work together, smoothly and securely.

System architects and designers work for software companies, IT companies, large engineering firms, telecommunication companies, and financial institutions. To work as a computer systems architect or designer, you will need to be familiar with many programming languages and operating systems. Some companies keep systems designers on staff, but most are hired on contract. When the job is complete, they often offer extra technical support through telecommuting. You won't start out as a systems architect or designer. You will begin as a coder and work your way up.

Job Titles for Computer Systems Designers

⇨ Computer Systems Design Engineer

⇨ Computer Systems Engineer

⇨ Computer Software Engineer

⇨ Systems Analyst

What Computer Systems Architects and Designers Do

⇨ They meet with clients to figure out what the company needs.

⇨ They decide which systems will work best for each client.

⇨ They write code that allows the new system to work with any existing software.

⇨ They organize upgrades, so the new system is up and running with as little interruption to workers as possible.

⇨ They write user-friendly training manuals.

⇨ They test and retest the system to make sure it works efficiently.

⇨ They write new code to fix problems or expand how the software is used.

\<Spotlight/\>

Alan Turing (1912–1954), Father of Theoretical Computer Science and Artificial Intelligence

Alan Turing was born in London, England, on June 23, 1912. His father worked for the British government in India, and throughout their childhoods, Turing and his brother, John, were often left in the care of family friends.

At the age of six, Turing started school, and almost immediately, his teachers recognized his genius. When he was thirteen, he was accepted into Sherborne School, a private school for boys. When the 1926 General Strike threatened to keep him from attending his first day of class, he hopped on his bicycle and rode, alone, the sixty miles to school, staying one night in an inn along the way.

After graduation from Sherborne, he attended Kings College in Cambridge and graduated with high honors in mathematics. In 1931, using the work of Kurt Gödel, he proved that a machine was capable of preforming any mathematical equation so long as it was presented as an algorithm, a step-by-step set of specific instructions. This hypothetical machine was called the Turing Machine. And the idea of the modern computer was born!

While attending Princeton University in the United States, Turing studied mathematics and cryptography, which is the reading and writing of secret messages or codes, and earned a PhD. His study of cryptography proved helpful when, in 1939, he returned to England and World War II began.

Throughout the war, Turing worked at Bletchley Park, where the British government housed their Code and

Cypher School. The school did top-secret work that led to the breaking of Germany's Enigma and Lorenz codes. Turing and his team's work is credited with changing the outcome of the war, shortening it by two to four years and saving over fourteen million lives. In 1945, Turing was awarded the Order of the British Empire, but his contributions to the war effort were kept a secret and not recognized until many years later.

In the mid-1940s, Turing worked at the National Physical Laboratory in Middlesex on a design for an Automatic Computing Engine. He presented his work in a paper dated February 19, 1946, and in that paper, he described in detail the first stored-program computer.

In 1948, Turing joined the mathematics department at the University of Manchester. A year later, he became deputy director of the Royal Society Computing Machine Laboratory and began writing software for one of the first stored-program computers—the Manchester Mark 1. He continued his work at the university until his death on June 7, 1954, from possible cyanide poisoning. He was almost forty-two years old.

<Computer Systems Programmers/>

Systems programmers create and maintain the operating system that acts as each computer's brain. Like any brain, the operating system controls how the computer acts. Written in the code are directions for how the computer will handle software applications, store data, manage demands on memory, interact with elements like the keyboard and mouse, and interact with other machines like printers, scanners, or cameras.

Systems programmers write code in low-level programming languages called machine code or assembly code. They work for computer manufacturers, systems software houses, and the military. Companies that hire systems programmers choose those with bachelor's degrees in subjects like computer science, computer engineering, microelectronics, physics, or mathematics.

Common Operating Systems

Android: Based on Linux software, Android was developed by Google and is designed for use in touch-screen mobile devices like smartphones and tablets. It is also used in smart televisions, cars, cameras, game consoles, and wristwatches. The system uses touch, like tapping, swiping, and pinching, to perform tasks and work a virtual keyboard.

IBM z/OS: This is a 64-bit operating system used in IBM mainframe computers. Mainframe computers are usually owned by corporations or governments for important work like bank transactions, tax return information, census data processing, and other uses that require manipulating humongous amounts of information.

iOS: This operating system is used exclusively on Apple mobile devices.

Linux: A free, open source software used in servers for business and on workstations at universities and engineering companies, it was created by Linus Torvalds, then a college student from Helsinki, Finland. This operating system was used to produce the movie *Titanic*. It powered the graphics, which were a big part of the movie's success.

Microsoft Windows: This family of graphical operating systems developed by Microsoft allows the user to interact with the computer using graphics rather than text.

OS X: This is the main operating system for all Apple Macintosh computers.

QNX: This is commonly used in embedded systems, which are designed for a specific task. Embedded systems are used in small devices like digital watches and MP3 players and in large devices like traffic lights and hybrid cars.

UNIX: This family of operating systems can trace its origins to AT&T's UNIX system that was developed at Bell Laboratories in the 1970s.

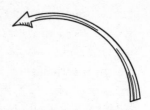

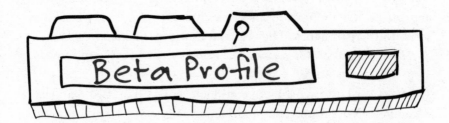

Name: Anne Zepecki
Age: 16
Job (when not studying!): Creator, Girls Learn to Code

When did you first discover that you were interested in writing code?

I have lived my whole life in Silicon Valley, surrounded by some of the most successful and well-known tech companies. My father, aunt, and grandfather all have engineering/computer science degrees. With this background, I was naturally very interested in what it was that these companies and my family members were actually doing. It wasn't until the summer before my eighth grade year, when I attended AAUW's [American Association of University Women] Tech Trek! and got to hear Danielle Feinberg talking about how computer science applies to Pixar movies, that I was really interested in learning how to code.

How did you learn to write code, and what language(s) do you know?

I learned how to code when I was a sophomore in high school in my AP [advanced placement] computer science class. Before then, I didn't have any true coding experience, but I have been interested in math and science from a young age. In that class, I learned how to code in Java.

During the summer after my sophomore year, I took a summer quarter class at Stanford University in client-side technology. It was there where I learned how to code websites using the markup languages HTML and CSS, as well as learning to code in Java-Script. Currently, I am teaching myself how to code in Python.

You are working on a website to help girls become interested in computer science. Describe your site and what you hope to achieve with it.

I decided to create my website, which is called Girls Learn Code (girlslearncode.com), because I wanted to try and find a way to present coding and computer science to teenage girls in a more appealing way and to attract more females to the field at a younger age. Though there have been some wonderful outreach programs, both on the national and local level, there are not a lot of resources for girls who want to get a glimpse of what computer science is like and learn the very basics of what coding is and how to code. With my site, I aim to provide girls with an overview of what coding is, the basics of coding in Java, and what they can do with coding. I want to get them interested enough in computer science that they will choose to pursue the topic in more depth.

My site includes several components. First off, there are fifteen interactive, beginning-level lessons in Java, which is the language taught in AP computer science. The lessons are short and quick enough that the user can complete one in about five minutes or so, including the review questions that aid the user in truly digesting and retaining what it is she is learning. There is also a projects page on the site, which includes the resources to complete an independent project written in Java using a real compiler, as well as instructions on how to do some basic actions in HTML, the markup language used to code websites.

The projects in HTML are how to make your own slideshow and how to create a shape on the web page that you can move around. My favorite page on the site is the Computer Science in the Real World page. On this page, girls see different areas of interest, such as sports, music, or movies, and can read about how computer science applies to the field. I created this specific page because a lot of the girls that I have talked to believe that computer science is a field that does not touch people on a day-to-day basis, aside from through technological devices like smartphones or computers.

There is a Resources page on the website that gives a list of organizations that girls can look to, so that they can keep exploring computer science, whether through camps and activities or by simply learning more about coding.

I plan to keep on revising the site over the next few years. You could call my current work a first draft. I want to update the graphics, include more lessons in Java, and have a greater number of sample questions and projects.

Can you explain the process you go through to design, define, and then launch a website?
Designing a website is very interesting. First, I wrote down on paper sketches of what I wanted the basic layout of each page to look like: what components I would have, what colors things would be, and how things would be arranged on the page. From there, I tried to implement my basic plan for each page into an HTML file. A lot of my original ideas ended up being revised when I discovered that the layouts I designed looked different on the screen than on paper. It was interesting to watch how the graphic design of the site morphed into what it is now.

Another big part of the design process was determining the content. I wrote all of the lessons in Java myself, based on my knowledge of the language (but I did check to make sure the information was accurate). Presenting complex information in a simple, engaging way is difficult, so I did a lot of research on how people learn and how to most effectively teach. I decided on short lessons so that the user could just sit down and quickly learn something new, and included lots of review questions so that the lessons would be retained.

To implement my ideas, I used the markup language CSS for all of the colors, alignment, fonts, and other style elements; the actual components of the site like the words and images were part of the HTML code. Going into the project, I already knew quite a bit about how to code a website because I had had a summer of practice, so most of the things I needed I already knew. However, online resources were great for brushing up on my skills and for making sure I was using the right syntax and tags. In HTML, you have things called tags that are denoted by a letter or word surrounded by two chevron symbols. For example, <p>Hello!</p> denotes a paragraph (abbreviated as p) that reads, "Hello!"

Once I finished putting all of the content on the pages, it was time to take the site live. I had to purchase a domain, or URL, to put the site up so everyone can see it. After that, I had to make sure all of my pages were linked to one another. In order to do that, I had to make sure that they were in the correct folders, and then I had to write basic code in the files for each page that locally (on the computer/site) linked the correct page to the different buttons and links. After doing this, my files were a lot more organized, and I was ready to go.

It was pretty simple to upload my files onto my site and then go live! One of the coolest experiences of my life was when I first saw something that I had created on the web available for anyone to see. It's the neatest feeling to look at something and be able to say, "Yeah, I made that." It makes you feel like all of your hard work turned into something better than you could have ever expected.

Why do you think it's important for girls to look at computer science as a career choice?
Because our world needs more women in coding, and women can bring a lot to the field. Some studies I have read have found that women are most interested in the social impact that their work in computer science can have. More women in computer science could help create a better future.

There are a lot of jobs that will open up over the next ten years that are all tech related, and in order to keep up with the industry, we need to have new minds in the workforce that can provide new ideas, solutions, and innovations to our world. Women are a virtually untapped resource in the field. They can bring a lot and can help engineer the next technological advances that will enable society to excel.

How do you balance your schoolwork with all your other activities?

Sometimes, it can be difficult to balance all of my activities with my schoolwork, but what usually works best for me is prioritizing. I make a list of everything I need to do with the most important things at the top and the least urgent at the bottom. I go through my list and get done as much of it as I can each day. I find that this system works really well for me. Also, I try to stay focused while I am doing my work so that I can get everything accomplished; this means avoiding the temptations of social media and Netflix, mostly.

Where do you see yourself in ten years?

Working in the tech industry. I want to work for a company that gives back to society in some way. I want to have a positive impact on society with the work I do. After that, I eventually hope to have a family and maybe even teach computer science so that I can share what I love to do with others.

010010010010010010010010010010010010010010010

Applications Programmers

Applications programmers write software that is installed on every computer to do different tasks like word processing, document design, bookkeeping, email, and security. More programmers are employed to work with applications than with systems.

Applications, called apps when referring to those used on mobile devices, are software programs written to perform a specific task.

You install an application on a device, and it runs inside the operating system until you close it. Most of the time, there is more than one application running at a time. Running multiple applications is called multitasking.

<Software Developers/>

One of the more creative coding jobs is that of the software developer. These people design and write the code that allows people to do a wide variety of tasks on their computers or mobile devices. Some develop the underlying systems that run the devices while others write the programs that are used on the device. Many software developers work for computer systems design firms, software publishers, and large corporations like Intel or Boeing.

What Software Developers Do

⇨ Take an idea and analyze what the user will need.

⇨ Design the software structure to meet those needs.

⇨ Write the software.

⇨ Test and retest the software and fix problems.

⇨ Plan how each software program will interact with other programs.

⇨ Create flowcharts, models, or diagrams to teach programmers how to write the code.

⇨ Maintain and test periodically to be sure the program is performing properly.

⇨ Document everything they do so someone else can understand what they did.

Software developers understand the big picture. They oversee the writing of a software program from start to finish. Once the program is done, they are the ones who fix any flaws in the code, including making it more user-friendly. Once the program is released, they also write upgrades and maintenance code.

<Computer Programmers, aka Coders/>

Computer coders spend most of their days writing code. They take what the software developer designed and turn it into code that the computer can understand. To work as a programmer, you will need an associate's degree and some experience or a bachelor's degree. Most programmers focus on knowing a few programming languages very well. Computer programmers often work alone or on small teams, and some telecommute. They are hired to work in many industries, including hospitals, schools, web-based companies, and the government.

What Coders Do

⇨ Write the code for a program using a variety of computer languages.

⇨ Monitor programs and write updates to fix problems.

⇨ Write code that expands a program's functions.

⇨ Test and fix errors in the code. This is called debugging.

⇨ Write and use tools that automate some of the writing process.

⇨ Collect into code libraries any lines of code that simplify specific tasks.

Job Areas for Coders

⇨ Web development and design

⇨ Desktop applications

⇨ Games, animation, and 3-D graphics

⇨ Applications for mobile devices

⇨ Scientific and engineering applications

⇨ Business and education applications

The World's Five Fastest Computers

1. Tianhe-2: China's supercomputer is the fastest in the world. It runs at 33.86 petaflops (a petaflop is a thousand trillion floating-point operations per second. The computer is housed in the Shenzhen's National Supercomputing Centre in Shenzhen, China, where it's used by universities and Chinese companies.

2. Titan: The United States' fastest supercomputer is housed at the Oak Ridge National Labs in Oakridge, Tennessee. It runs at 17.6 petaflops and consumes less energy than much smaller computers.

3. Sequoia: This IBM Blue Gene design runs at 17.17 petaflops and is used for nuclear explosion simulations. Sequoia is housed at the Lawrence Livermore National Laboratory in Livermore, California.

4. K-Computer: Japan's supercomputer runs at 10.5 petaflops. It is housed at the RIKEN Advanced Institute for Computational Science in Kobe, Japan.

5. Mira Blue Gene: This IBM design runs at 8.6 petaflops. It is housed at the United States' Argonne National Laboratory in Lemont, Illinois.

<Desktop Applications Coders/>

Desktop applications coders write code that is used on desktops or laptops. These applications include word processing software like Microsoft Word, spreadsheet software like Apple Numbers, and presentation software like Microsoft Publisher. They also write software that businesses use to track customer information, monitor inventory, and pay bills. Applications coders typically write programs in high-level languages. They must be able to think logically and communicate with a variety of technical and business people.

Types of Desktop Applications

⇨ Word processing software is used to create a variety of documents like letters, posters, or greeting cards. The most common one is Microsoft Word.

⇨ Web browser software is the tool you use to access the internet. Some are already installed on the computer, but you can download any one you prefer. Examples are Internet Explorer, Chrome, and Mozilla Firefox.

⇨ Game applications abound. From card games to action-packed shoot-'em-up games, almost any kind is available.

⇨ Media players are used to listen to music or watch movies. Examples are VLC Media Player or iTunes.

<Mobile Apps Coders/>

Mobile apps coders and developers design apps that are used on smaller handheld devices like smartphones and tablets. They have to be con-stantly learning and adapting to new mobile usage rules. Unlike desktop applications, mobile apps are designed for the smaller screen and must be user-friendly while still giving the user access to the information they want.

Mobile coders work for large businesses, tech companies, and any smaller organization that wants to engage with their customers or clients in on-the-go real-time. Some work independently while others work for consulting companies. They often write code using Objective-C or Java, and HTML/CSS for mobile websites.

Developing Your Own App

As the market gets flooded with mobile apps, it will take a creative and innovative idea to break into the market. If you think you have an amazing app idea, there are four ways you can sell it:

➡ Sell it on your own website and hope that people find it.

➡ Sell it to a larger company. If it's amazing, this could happen.

➡ Get it listed in an app store. Watch out! The application process can be hard, but you can do it.

➡ Open source it so others can use it. You won't make money, but you'll have it for your portfolio.

Microsoft has developed a kid-friendly programming language called TouchDevelop. By simply tapping the touch screen on a Microsoft mobile phone, you can connect blocks of code and build a mobile app of your very own.

Types of Mobile Apps

➡ News apps like Flipboard allow you to create your own news feed. You get to choose the type of stories you want to see and the app chooses articles and delivers the content to your device.

➡ Encyclopedia apps like Wolfram|Alpha are huge encyclopedias that can answer almost any question you ask. There are also smaller apps that focus on specific subjects like science or math.

⇨ Radio apps like TuneIn Radio allow you to stream podcasts, talk radio, or music stations from anywhere in the world, anytime you have internet access.

⇨ Health apps like S Health help you track your exercise, count calories, watch your weight, and monitor other health issues.

⇨ Banking apps like those from Wells Fargo or Bank of America allow you to check your balances, deposit checks remotely, and transfer funds from one account to another.

Quiz
The Matching Game

Match the programmer to the job description.

1. Scientific Programmer	A. I write codes that govern the natural laws of a real or pretend world. How high does a ball bounce? How fast does a car sink into mud? How far can a launched chicken fly?
2. High-Performance Programmer	B. I write applications on which people can compose a letter, design a birthday card, or keep track of their spending.
3. Mobile Programmer	C. I write codes that allow people to play online games together. I also write codes that keep servers secure and help prevent cheating.
4. Front-End Developer	D. I write games like *Angry Birds* or *Candy Crush Saga*. I also write applications that help people find a good restaurant, check the weather, or share photos with friends.
5. Desktop Applications Programmer	E. I have about ten years of experience writing code. I work for scientists who want to model the structure of a cell, study climate change, or study the origins of the universe.

6. Game Programmer	F. I make websites look great and work well.
7. Network Programmer	G. I work with huge amounts of data. I write programs for banks that handle lots of money, for the US Census Bureau when they want to crunch a lot of numbers, or for the FBI's facial recognition system.
8. Artificial Intelligence Programmer	H. I write the codes that define fantasy worlds and make people's avatars look and act real.
9. Physics Engine Programmer	I. I write software that converts source code, which programmers can read, into object code, which machines can read.
10. Compiler Programmer	J. I write software that controls robots, helps doctors diagnose patients, or allows computers to interact with people.

Mainframe, Embedded Software, and Firmware Coders

Two bytes meet. The first byte looks at the other and says, "You don't look like yourself today. Are you feeling okay?" The second byte replies, "No, I feel a *bit* off."

You live in a fast-paced, quickly changing world where all of your devices—computers, tablets, smartphones, smart televisions, smart refrigerators, medical devices, and cars—are interconnected. They talk to each other. They talk to you. And they quickly and easily pass along massive amounts of information. All this interconnectivity is called the Internet of Things (IoT), and it is driven by the skills and imagination of computer coders around the world.

The term *Internet of Things* refers to the increasing number of things that are connected to the internet by sensors and devices that transmit information. The first internet-connected machine was a Coke dispenser at Carnegie Mellon University. It was put online in 1982 and could send inventory and temperature information to a computer.

A "thing" in the IoT can be a car with built-in GPS, a cow with sensors embedded under the skin that track her movements, or an athlete wearing an armband that keeps a log of his or her heart rate and workout level.

Capturing Proton Collisions!

With the help of coders, scientists at the Large Hadron Collider discovered the Higgs boson particle (aka the God Particle) in 2013. The particle was found when two protons collided, emitting the particle. The machine they used created one million proton-to-proton collisions every second, but only one in every ten trillion collisions actually produces this particle. To store and process all that collision data, scientists would have needed more computing power than all the world's computers combined. To reduce the amount of data, coders created a trigger, which was made using a combination of hardware and software. The trigger fires each time there is an important collision and the data must be saved. If it doesn't fire, the collision data is lost forever. The trigger uses many strategies to decide whether a collision looks interesting enough to save. Since the trigger is only as smart as its code, if the code is wrong, a new discovery could be lost forever. No pressure there!

The IoT is an unregulated system in which data is easily collected and used without human interaction. For example, car insurance companies can gather data about a driver's habits. Does the person drive over the speed limit? Brake suddenly? Take corners too fast? All of this data can then be used to determine insurance rates.

How can so many items be connected to the internet at one time? Each sensor has an IP address that is specific to that thing. With the implementation of Internet Protocol Version 6 (IPv6), there are enough IP addresses to assign one to every atom on the surface of planet Earth—one hundred times! We won't be running out of them anytime soon.

As the IoT grows, so do concerns about the privacy of data and how that data should be used. Although the media tends to focus on internet-connected refrigerators and other things that seem benign, the IoT is being used right now by insurance companies, health providers, and other businesses. The government and private firms are working to establish guidelines and laws to keep everyone's information safe. The issues of identity theft, personal privacy, and discrimination must be addressed in the near future.

The first company dedicated to the production of mainframe computers was the Electronic Controls Company, later renamed Eckert-Mauchly Computer Corporation (EMCC). It was founded by J. Presper Eckert and John Mauchly in 1949.

Name: Spencer Glazer
Age: 16
Job (when not studying!): Video Game Creator

When did you first discover that you were interested in writing code?

At an early age, I had no knowledge of why or how my favorite games worked. When I was in junior high, I was told that video games and other electronics that allowed our society to function were able to work through coding. This excited me beyond anything I had ever heard before. Thus, I began to learn about this fantastic skill.

How did you learn to write code, and what language(s) do you know?

My high school has a coding club where we learn about various coding languages and coded devices. We have a license for Code Academy, which allows us to learn many languages such as C+ and Python.

Describe your experiences working with Arduino boards. [Those are tiny computer boards used to create devices that interact with their environment.]

I have basic experience with Arduino boards, and I have made a few projects such as an oscillating light, but I plan to dive into new endeavors such as clapping lights or clocks.

Describe your experiences creating video games.

I participated in an educational video game workshop run by Pepperdine University where I made a game through an online tool known as Twine. I created a text-based game while others in the workshop made side-scrolling or overhead games. In Coding Club, we are able to go online and look for other game creation software, and our school has a license to use Kodu on all of our computers.

I made a text-based game about an isolated creature in a primeval world struggling to find its species. I also helped others who participated in the video game creation workshop with their games. One of theirs was an overhead game where you had to avoid many minuscule projectiles.

What do you think is the key to creating a great video game?

The idea. You have to have an amazing idea to excite you and inspire you to work as hard as you possibly can. The idea lets the creator plan and make new ideas based off that. Everything is important to create a great game, but without an underlying idea, nothing can be created.

Why you think teamwork is important as you are learning to write code?
Peers can inspire and challenge us, and keep us excited about a project. If just one person codes by themselves, they can grow bored and frustrated, but a peer alongside them could challenge them with their own work and give them new ideas for their next project. That is why I still code and my friends do too.

How do you balance your schoolwork with all your other activities?
I work hard. That is my miracle cure. Hard work can overcome any obstacle. I also know where my priorities are. I put what is a necessity first and everything else second, so I can get all my important tasks done. I also know how much I can do. If you do not know your limits, then you will eventually burn out. A regular eight hours of sleep doesn't hurt either.

Where do you see yourself in ten years?
I honestly have no idea. I have not decided on my primary college or major yet. I feel as though I still have time, but I do know that in ten years, I will have coding knowledge to carry me into an amazing career.

0100100100100100100100100100100100100010010010

Mainframe Coders

Mainframe computers, affectionately known as Big Iron, are those supercomputers that are huge, expensive, reliable, and megafast! They are owned by governments, large corporations, banks, and any business that collects a lot of data or processes a lot of transactions. Mainframe computers are built for speed but must be reliable, secure, process massive amounts of data, and run without interruption for decades. An up-and-coming task of mainframe computers is to support the emerging use of the cloud.

About 80 percent of the United States' most profitable companies rely on mainframes. Their computers have decades of programming work written in COBOL and assembler languages on them. That means that they are complex, and the need for experienced COBOL programmers to maintain them is not going away anytime soon. According to Compuware, "One minute of mainframe outages can cost nearly $14,000 in lost revenue for an average enterprise [company]."[1]

Although new mainframe computer code for businesses is not being written in COBOL, the need for programmers who write in the language is increasing. As the baby boomer generation enters retirement, their jobs are not being replaced by younger COBOL programmers. It is a language that is not being taught everywhere, so if you are interested in learning it, you'll have to make sure your school offers classes.

And don't forget Fortran. Scientific programs at many research institutions and universities were written using it. Those systems will also need coders to maintain them.

\<Spotlight/\>

Konrad Zuse (1910–1995), Father of the Programmable Computer

Konrad Zuse was born in Berlin, Germany, but moved to East Prussia when he was only two years old. The family lived in Braunsberg, where his father worked for the postal service, and Zuse attended the local Jesuit school. When he was thirteen, the family moved to Hoyerswerda, Germany, where he attended Realschule, a school that allowed students to continue their studies at one of several technical universities.

After passing his secondary school exams, Zuse entered the Technical University of Berlin. He dabbled in mechanical engineering and architecture coursework but found both areas of study boring. In 1935, he graduated with a degree in civil engineering and went to work for the Henschel Aircraft Company in Berlin. At the aircraft factory, he was forced to perform repetitive mathematical calculations until he felt he would go insane. He dreamed of a future where this tedious task could be done by a machine.

While living with his parents in their apartment in Berlin, he invented the Z1, the first electrically driven, mechanical calculator that was programmed using punched 35 mm movie film. It had thirty thousand parts but, unfortunately, never worked very well.

Throughout World War II, Zuse continued to work on other designs. First, the Z2, which was completed in 1939, kept the same memory as the Z1 but added electrical relay circuits. Then, the Z3, which was completed in 1941, became the world's first programmable, fully automatic, electromechanical computer. Unfortunately, the first three Z machines were destroyed during World War II. The Z3 and its blueprints were destroyed in an Allied raid in late 1943, and the Z1 and Z2, along with Zuse's parents' apartment, were destroyed in a British air raid on January 30, 1944.

Despite the loss of his first three computers, Zuse continued to work on the Z4. The war ended in 1945, and the misery of life in postwar Germany brought his work to a halt, not to be resumed until 1949. He finally sold his first Z4, a very reliable computer, to a Swiss university in 1950. The Z4 was the first commercially sold computer and, for a time, the only working digital computer in continental Europe.

In the mid-1940s, Zuse developed the first high-level programming language, Plankalkül, or Plan Calculus, written for a computer.

The Cloud

The cloud refers to those areas online where you can store software and other information on the servers of a third-party company, rather than on your personal computer or a company's server. The term *cloud computing* was coined by Compaq engineers in 1996, and the idea has been growing ever since. Today, the idea of "saving it to the cloud" has taken wings, and everyone is considering ways to use it. Photos posted to social media, documents saved on Google Drive, music bought on iTunes—these are examples of how the cloud is entering our everyday lives.

For coders, the cloud offers an easy way to collaborate. There are several sites that allow programmers to work on each other's code and send feedback, even from great distances. GitHub is one of the most popular sites and is sometimes called a social networking site for coders. GitHub stores copies of code from the first draft to the final edit. This "version control system" allows coders to easily return to previous versions if they make a mistake. It also allows other coders to learn new ways of solving problems. GitHub allows programmers to download copies of the code, make changes, and send the changes to the original creator of the code. The original creator can then decide whether to merge those changes or not. This allows for greater collaboration between programmers even when they live in different countries.

Cloud computing has also made learning to code easier. With platform as a service technology (PaaS), students can learn to code on a web browser, rather than downloading the software to their computer. Many of these programs also provide a terminal as well as a text editor on the same screen, allowing programmers to see the effects of their code without switching screens.

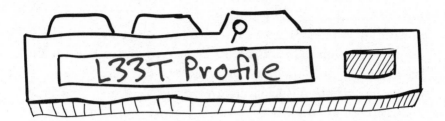

Name: Paul Mitchell
Job: Senior firmware engineer, Starkey Hearing Technologies

When did you first become interested in writing computer code and decide to make it the focus of your career?
While in junior high, I remember sending some simple Fortran programs into work with my father. I would get a listing with the program code and any output the program produced. At that point, I hadn't been introduced to batch processing of programs on a mainframe—that detail was handled by my dad. I would learn that later in my computer science courses at the University of Minnesota. Later, while at the university, it became clear that I was good at programming and it was something I enjoyed doing.

What education/work path did you take to get where you are today?
Some of my programming languages were self-taught, starting with Fortran. The first algorithm I learned was a bubble sort taught in high school. Later, at the university, I learned how inefficient that bubble sort really was. The bulk of my knowledge comes from on-the-job experience. I also take continuing education courses to keep on top of the latest techniques, tools, and so forth.

You began programming in the 1970s. Describe what the process was like back then.
In high school, we used a time-share system. We had to dial a phone number and connect to the time-share system through a modem. To use this modem, the telephone receiver was

physically placed into the modem. Direct input and output to the time-share system was through the use of a TTY-33 teletype device. Also, there was a card reader attached. This card reader didn't read punched cards but cards marked with a pencil. We used BASIC when programming with that time-share system.

When I was in college, we used a batch processing system. This is where punched cards were used. We got to punch our own cards, but at large companies, you could actually make money punching cards. These systems used the standard eighty-column punched cards. (At the time, IBM also produced a ninety-six-column small punch card).

I also worked as a technician for a company that made high-speed test equipment for computer memory chips. The chips were used in mainframes and mini-computers. Part of my job was to write simple programs for the microprocessor that tested the machine. To do that, we would use machine language to create simple programs (routines) using switches and push buttons. We could step though the program one instruction at a time and view the results on the LEDs [light emitting diodes— tiny light bulbs] on the face of the box. Once the system was up and running, further programming was performed using the CRT [cathode-ray tube: a computer monitor and a keyboard] and floppy drives.

Describe the kind of programming work you have done, including what languages you know.

In the early days of networking computers, I used a bulk file transfer program that was written in a dialect of Fortran-77. I also used a diagnostic program for the networking adapter (hardware) written in Algol and a device driver for the networking adapter written in assembler.

With a team of others, I've worked on programming medical equipment. The device is used in a doctor's office during follow-up visits, after a pacemaker is implanted. The device is used to read diagnostic information from the pacemaker. This diagnostic data is used by the clinician or doctor to determine if any changes in therapy are required. The number of safety protocols and interlocks in the hardware was interesting. This rather large project was written in C++. I've also worked on a small, handheld unit that is used by a patient to modify which pain therapy program is used by an implantable pain management device. Being a small, battery-powered handheld device, the firmware was written in C.

And then there was the White Bear Tech pet location product. By using GPS modules and radios, the product was able to determine the relative position of the collar with respect to the handheld unit. The firmware for this product needed to talk to numerous hardware blocks and use various algorithms to convert the raw measurements into usable data. Other algorithms were generated to help draw screens on the LCD display, presenting, to the user, a visual representation of the relative position between the two. All this firmware was written in C++.

Over the years, most of the projects I worked on were coded in either C or C++. This is mostly due to the domain that the projects fell in; if, for example, the projects had been web applications, the programming languages would have been different.

You have worked on contract and as a direct hire. What do you see as the advantages and disadvantages of each?
In general, contractors are hired for the tools and the technologies they know. As a contractor, you need to continue learning new tools and technologies to remain relevant and hireable. If you like learning new skills, this would be one way to go. The new skill can either be learned on the job or independently. Of course, there is less job security and usually longer hours (contractors are hired when projects are behind schedule), and it pays more with fewer benefits.

Direct hires are expected to know (or learn) the company's product domain. The company will train you on the other tools that are used during product development. While pay is less than a contractor's, there are more benefits, the possibility of advancement, team bonding, and so forth.

Coders are creative people and often want to take their ideas and start their own company. You started White Bear Tech. Can you describe your experiences?

White Bear Tech produced the pet location devices I mentioned before. The technology would allow the owner to track a pet up to about one mile away. The pet collar and the handheld unit contained a radio and GPS. The two units talked to each other. With a compass in the handheld to orientate the screen, the user would get a visual indication of the pet's location.

When starting a company, you get to pick a fun idea for a product, or a product that you can become emotionally invested in. Getting together with a small group of friends or acquaintances, assigning roles to get the product to market can be enjoyable.

The feel of working at a start-up company is different. It feels more informal, where everyone knows, respects, and trusts each other. And the work conditions can be more flexible.

However, as you can guess, since there is pressure to get the product out to the market, there can also be interpersonal conflicts. Other pressures include being underfunded and coming up with the next great idea.

What do you see in the future for computer programming and/or for programmers?

This is a hard question to answer. This field changes so quickly. It is also cyclical. For example, for a while AI [artificial intelligence] was a hot area; then it cooled down. Now it is hot again, with Google and others looking for people with AI experience. Then there are new fields, such as the Internet of Things.

What advice would you give, tips for success, to a young person who is interested in becoming a programmer?

Programs and projects are becoming more complex. And the field is becoming more mature. Collaboration between teams of programmers requires a common language, such as design patterns (e.g., bridge pattern), collaboration tools for source code control, code inspections, pair programming, and so forth.

While honing your programming skills, also work on your interteam skills. Like any professional occupation, you want to keep up on your skill set throughout your career.

0100100100100100100100100100100100100010010010

Embedded Systems and Firmware Coders

The IoT would not be possible without the skills of programmers who write the code that drives each device. Every "thing" on the IoT has software written specifically for it. The code, called firmware, is loaded onto read-only memory, or flash memory chips, that become part of the device.

Firmware, after it is written, uploaded, and placed in a device, becomes part of an embedded system. Embedded systems are used whenever there is a repetitive task. The tasks can be simple or complex. And there are some tasks that don't really look repetitive, but they are—think of the firmware in a hearing aid and all the signal processing that it does.

Embedded systems are in dishwashers, microwaves, cameras, and printers. In devices like these, the code is not reprogrammable. In other systems—like robots in assembly plants, mobile phones, and the safety computer in cars and trucks—the code is reprogrammable. If there is a problem with the performance in one of these devices, a programmer can rewrite the code and upload it, thus fixing the problem. This is called a firmware upgrade.

You are probably most familiar with the firmware upgrades that happen on your mobile phone. Here are a few really awesome firmware upgrades that you may not have heard about:

⇨ In 2010, NASA upgraded the firmware on Voyager 2, which was over nine billion miles from Earth.

⇨ In 2012, NASA upgraded the firmware on the Mars Science Laboratory's rover Curiosity. They transmitted the data while it was hurtling through space at eight thousand mph.

⇨ In 2014, the European Space Agency upgraded the firmware on the Philae lander. The lander was 407 million miles from Earth, near Comet 67P/Churyumov-Gerasimenko, and traveling at eleven thousand mph. It is part of the Rosetta mission, which is the first space mission to meet up with a comet, follow it as it orbits the sun, and put a lander on the surface.

Programming the Giant Brain

In 1946, six women were hired to work on a secret World War II project for the US Army in Philadelphia. Their task was to program the Electronic Numerical Integrator and Computer (ENIAC). It was fondly known as the Giant Brain because it was an eight-foot-tall, eighty-foot-long machine. These brilliant women were the first to work as full-time computer programmers. Without the use of manuals or programming languages, they programmed a computer that could run complex equations in seconds, a feat that was unheard of at the time.

These six women, whose story was lost to history for over fifty years, dedicated their lives to making programming easier for the next generation. The team included Kay McNulty, Betty Jennings, Betty Snyder, Marlyn Wescoff, Fran Bilas, and Ruth Lichterman. Their story is told in a documentary titled *The Computers*.

<Embedded Software Engineers/>

Skills that companies look for:

⇨ A bachelor's or master's degree in software engineering or a related field

⇨ Software development experience

⇨ Excellent C and C++ language skills

- ⇨ Strong math skills

- ⇨ Strong debugging and problem-solving skills

- ⇨ Know-how to work with revision control and issue tracking systems

- ⇨ Strong documentation and writing skills

\<Firmware Engineers/\>

Skills that companies look for:

- ⇨ A bachelor's degree in physics, mathematics, or electrical engineering

- ⇨ Programming experience, especially in Java, C, C++

- ⇨ Microsoft SQL Server experience

- ⇨ A firmware engineering certificate from a recognized school

- ⇨ Knowledge of the Linux operating system

- ⇨ Ability to work in a team

Quiz: Name That Coder Movie

Quiz

1. A thirteen-year-old wins a computerized home. In order to keep his dad from falling in love with the computer programmer, he reprograms the home to do all the household chores but with disastrous consequences.

   A. *Smart House*

   B. *The iHome*

   C. *Mega Maid*

   D. *Keeping Up with the Coopers*

2. The makers of this animated movie, about a young robotics prodigy who must save the world with the help of his robot and four other friends, spent thirty-nine thousand hours creating a computer program that would render light more realistically.

   A. *Robo-kid*

   B. *Robots*

   C. *Big Hero 6*

   D. *The Incredible Robot*

3. This movie inspired Congress to create the Computer Fraud and Abuse Act of 1984. In the movie, a teenage computer whiz accidentally connects to the computer that controls the US nuclear arsenal. Thinking it's just an ordinary computer game, he then nearly starts World War III with Russia. Which movie was it?

   A. *WarGames*

   B. *World War 3.0*

   C. *Playing with Nukes*

   D. *Honey, I Destroyed the Planet*

4. After creating a computer virus, an eleven-year-old is banned from using a computer until he turns eighteen. Shortly after his eighteenth birthday, he and his friends must use their computer skills to stop the villain from spreading a dangerous new virus, all the while evading Secret Service agents.

   A. *Stop That Code!*

   B. *Hacking*

   C. *Hackers*

   D. *A Curious Code*

5. In this movie, a recent Stanford graduate lands his dream job at a software company with striking similarities to real–life Microsoft. However, he quickly discovers some ideas are deadly. Can he survive the workweek?

A. *Trust No One*

B . *Antitrust*

C. *Not-Software*

D. *SPAM*

6. A computer geek helps an experienced cop stop a terrorist who is trying to implement a fire sale—that is, a threefold cyberattack intended to cripple the nation's infrastructure.

A. *Geeks and Cops*

B. *Man on Fire*

C. *Live Free or Die Hard*

D. *Cowboys and Computer Coders*

7. Computer pioneer Alan Kay consulted with the screenwriter of this movie, which features a young man who gets trapped in a virtual game world.

A. *Tron*

B. *Virtual Escape*

C. *Finding X*

D. *Sharkboy and Lavagirl*

8. Creators of this movie about a group of security systems experts who are blackmailed into stealing an encryption device called on mathematician and leading encryption expert Len Adleman to consult on the story and make the props look realistic. Adleman agreed in exchange for his wife getting to meet Robert Redford, the star of the movie.

A. *The Box*

B. *Sneakers*

C. *Blackmail*

D. *Jeremiah Johnson*

9. The college student who created this documentary borrowed money from her dad to purchase the equipment she needed to create the movie. She filmed it on location at two different computer-hacking conventions.

A. *Let's Be Hackers*

B. *Hacking: The Documentary*

C. *Hacking Is Fun!*

D. *Hackers Are People Too*

10. The 2009 MythBusters episode "Car vs. Rain" featured a clip from this movie about two college students attempting to invent a high-powered laser.

A. *Smarty-pants*

B. *Bossy-boots*

C. *Real Genius*

D. *Laser Car!*

11. Filmmakers worked with Equifax.com to create a fake but fully-functioning version of the Equifax website for this movie. This was so the website would look and feel as real as possible. The film is about a head security officer for a bank who is forced to break down his own security systems in order to save his kidnapped family.

A. *Firewall*

B. *Security Breach*

C. *Double Agents*

D. *Taken*

12. In this movie, a computer whiz and two history buffs must save the Declaration of Independence from a group of unscrupulous treasure hunters. Fun fact—When looking for information, the good guys in the movie use Google, while the bad guys use the Yahoo! search engine.

A. *Declaration of Indepen-Dance*

B. *National Treasure*

C. *Code Breakers*

D. *The Road to El Dorado*

Video Games
and Animation

**Question: Why did the programmer get stuck
in the shower?**

ANSWER: BECAUSE THE INSTRUCTIONS ON THE SHAMPOO BOTTLE
SAID, "LATHER, RINSE, REPEAT."

Video Game Development

Video games fall into two categories. There are large, complex games like those played on a console or a computer. These games require a team to create and can take between eighteen and twenty-eight months to write. The others are smaller, less complex games like those played on mobile devices. Mobile games can be created in three to six months.

Whether a game is large or small, most go through a similar development process.

<Preproduction/>

Preproduction is when a game is born. Story ideas are narrowed down to one. Designers, with the help of artists and programmers, lay out the game's plot and their vision for any unique or exciting new elements. During preproduction, the game is divided into parts, and teams work on areas like storyline, software structure, and character development. Each team's work is gathered into a design document

that is used to create a prototype. The prototype process is where some design revisions take place. Prototypes are also used as sales tools to find publishers and get additional financing. Once a prototype is finished, production begins.

In China, they built a five-story apartment building using a 3-D printer. Instead of ink, this printer uses ground-up construction and industrial waste mixed with concrete. They also printed an 11,840-square-foot villa with all the decorative elements inside and out. With the help of creative coders, the sky's the limit on what a 3-D printer can create.

Production is when a game grows and matures. It is a time of intense collaboration. Teams of designers, artists, and programmers take the prototype and design documents and use them as guides for creating the final game. According to Louis Catanzaro, creative director for BeachCooler Games, "Art isn't displayed correctly until an [software] engineer makes it work, and it doesn't work until a designer defines how it should work."[2]

Designers decide how the game progresses, what happens on each level, and what the characters can and cannot do. Artists create drawings that show what different components look like including the main characters, landscapes, maps, vehicles, weapons or tools, and monsters or bad guys. Programmers build the game's software framework, including deciding how game elements will interact with each other and how the visual elements will be displayed.

Korea: The Gaming Mecca

Professional gaming in America is popular with a segment of the population, but in Korea, it's a part of the national culture. The Korean government introduced nationwide broadband internet in the late 1990s. Since then, playing games has become a national pastime, with live television broadcasts, tech company sponsors like Samsung and HTC, and celebrity players whose popularity rivals American football and basketball stars.

Professional gamers in both countries make about the same income. But in Korea, they are superstars who are recognized wherever they go. In Korea, there is a well-established network of gaming houses where players live and practice. In the United States, these are just starting to appear. In Korea, games are broadcast on television every day and pro gaming matches bring in huge advertising revenue. In the United States, games are seen on a limited number of stations.

And the Koreans are winning too! According to Korean player Chae "Piglet" Gwang-jin, the difference between Korean and American players is, "If someone [in the United States] plays thirty games a week—that's just a random number—a Korean would play seventy to eighty games. Take that difference over a week, over a month, over years, and that's going to be a huge difference."[1]

During production, the game goes through many revisions, each improving the design and adding depth and quality to the previous version. The production phase is finished once music and sound effects are added. This point in development is often celebrated and called "Content Complete!"

Video Game Genres

⇨ Hidden objects

⇨ Time management

⇨ Match three objects

⇨ Mahjong

⇨ Farm

⇨ Tycoon

⇨ Mystery

⇨ Adventure

⇨ Dress-Up

<Postproduction/>

Postproduction is when the game gets played and played and played. Game testers look for errors, document them, and pass them on for coders to fix. Testers also look for inconsistencies in the game or errors in content, characters, or storyline. Quality control people look for unanticipated moves a game player might make that the production teams missed. Dealing with all these fixes can take a lot of time, especially if the game is big and complex.

Once all the errors are fixed, the game is released. After release, game players often report issues they find. These issues are fixed and released via a patch or update. If the game is popular, there may be additional work done to expand it.

Beta Profile

Name: Jaime Herrera
Age: 17
Job (when not studying!): Founder and lead programmer,
Insanitygaming.net

When did you first discover that you were interested in writing code?

When my friends and family pushed me into the field of computers. I wanted to make video games. So I did some research and found that games were more than just images on a screen. If I wanted to make them, I would have to learn some coding. As I began to learn a few simple codes, I was able to see the objects I created do what I wanted them to do. I found that absolutely amazing!

How did you learn to write code, and what language(s) do you know?

By studying the codes of others. I learned some keywords so I could put my own codes together. This was also paired with many eBooks and questions to people who knew what they were doing. I am able to write in JavaScript and some C#, and I am learning to write in C++.

How did you come up with the idea for your first game, *Space Race: The Infinite?*

The idea came from necessity. Me and my original team—Steve Hartman (eighteen), Jeremiah Martin (eighteen), and Joshua Griffin (eighteen)—were looking for ways to be noticed, by anyone, really. We wanted to establish ourselves as people who were capable of creating our own original games. We did a lot of market research and found that infinite side-scrolling 2-D shooters were the most popular games at the time. Immediately, we set to work and created the game you see now.

I have also written a game called *The Night*. It is a first-person zombie-survival game that can be found on my website. [According to Insanitygaming.net, *The Night* is "a simple yet thrilling first-person zombie-survival simulator. Fight to slay as many zombies as possible before succumbing to the horde."]

How did you start your gaming company, Insanitygaming.net?

Working in the gaming industry has been a long-standing dream of mine and my friends. When we originally started, we wanted to be on the side of video gaming that the players were on. That still remains a goal for us; however, we are focused on the development side of video games for now. We started the company because as young, inexperienced indie [individual] developers, we would not be able to be hired by a company. Thus, Insanity Gaming was born. My goal for the company is to eventually be able to compete with larger companies like Nintendo or Bethesda.

Explain the process you go through to design, define, and then write a game.

The process of designing a game is actually quite simple. It starts with an idea. That idea is then presented to the entire team, and everyone provides their input. If the idea receives the okay, then we move on to design. This usually involves a vision for each character and the theme we would like to present with the game.

Once characters and the design have been set and drawn, we can start programming and animating. This is actually the longest part of the process, but it is only tedious because our team is small. Once the game is coded, we can look toward the platform we plan to publish on. A large factor in this is the processing power required to run the game. Typically, games that require a lot of processing power are reserved for PCs. Usually, we are able to determine the platforms we are going to release on when the idea for the game is presented.

How do you balance your schoolwork with all your other activities?

Balancing schoolwork with developing games, along with all other duties I must take on, has actually been fairly easy so far. I have been lucky and have had a lot of time and help from my team. Together, we are able to spread out the load of work so that no one person is overloaded.

0100100100100100100100100100100100100100010

<Jobs in Game Development/>

Developers know how to design games, write the programs, and create the artwork. Depending on the size of the game and the studio where it's being created, a developer may wear one or all of these hats. For large games in large companies, development may be many people working as a team. A developer's main goal is to create the best game possible.

Designers are the dreamers. The ones who imagine the look and feel of the game. Individually or as a team, they come up with ideas for storylines, characters, and game play. Once the ideas are collected, the team meets and chooses the best ones. During production, designers work with programmers and artists to make sure their design elements are carried throughout the game. Designers follow the programmers' work by viewing a prototype of the game. When changes need to be made, designers are on hand to help with that process.

Here are a few designer positions:

➪ **Lead designers** collect and organize ideas into a well-planned design document. They manage each team member's workload and schedule. They document progress, solve problems, and keep the game production on schedule.

➪ **Content designers** work on exciting twists and turns in the plot and create interesting, unique characters. They are responsible for consistency in the game's world. For example, if the game is set in the jungle, they make sure the plants and objects are consistent with a tropical environment—no snowstorms, no winter jackets, no lions or giraffes.

⇨ **Game mechanics designers** focus on the rules for how the game is played. They decide how the characters interact with each other and their environment. They decide how players pick up weapons, gain skills, or jump to the next level.

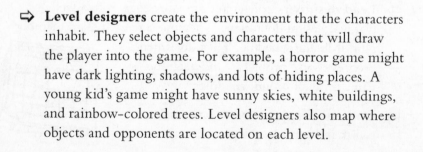

Ten Favorite Kids' Games

1. *Disney Infinity 2.0 Marvel Superheroes*

2. *Disney Magical World*

3. *LEGO Batman 3: Beyond Gotham*

4. *Little Big Planet 3*

5. *Mario Kart 8*

6. *Pokémon Art Academy*

7. *Pokémon Omega Ruby & Alpha Sapphire*

8. *PvZ: Garden Warfare*

9. *Skylanders Trap Team*

10. *Super Smash Bros*

⇨ **Level designers** create the environment that the characters inhabit. They select objects and characters that will draw the player into the game. For example, a horror game might have dark lighting, shadows, and lots of hiding places. A young kid's game might have sunny skies, white buildings, and rainbow-colored trees. Level designers also map where objects and opponents are located on each level.

⇨ **Writers** create the dialogue for each character. Role-playing games rely heavily on writers to create authentic interactions between characters. Puzzle or maze games don't require a writer.

\<Spotlight/\>

Saint Isidore, Bishop of Seville (560–636) Patron Saint of Computers, Programmers and the Internet

As a child, Isidore attended the Cathedral school of Seville where he was taught by many learned men, including his older brother, Archbishop Leander of Seville (who also became a saint). While there, Isidore was taught critical thinking skills through the study of factual information gleaned from the five senses: sight, sound, taste, touch, and smell. He also studied arithmetic, geometry, music, and astronomy, as well as Latin, Greek, and Hebrew.

After the death of his older brother, Isidore became the next archbishop of Seville. As archbishop, he saw himself as the protector of the people. To that end, he encouraged religious discipline and the assimilation of the various cultures in his jurisdiction into one united nation.

A man devoted to education, he used logical reasoning to fight the encroachment of Gothic barbarism into his domain. He encouraged the education movement in Seville and was the first to introduce his people to the work of the Greek philosopher Aristotle.

Isidore died in Seville on April 4, 636, at the age of seventy-six. His bones are buried in the Cathedral Church of Murcia. He was canonized a saint by the Roman Catholic

Church in 1598 by Pope Clement VIII, and declared a Doctor of the Church in 1722 by Pope Innocent XIII.

Today, he is best known for writing a twenty-volume encyclopedia, a dictionary, and a history of the world. Because of his work compiling knowledge into one collection—these books—the Catholic Church has named him the patron saint of computers, computer users, programmers, and the internet.

\<Coders/\>

Coders are visionaries who see a video game as lines of code that determine how a computer or mobile device will handle the game. They work with the design team and build the game, line by line of code, from the ground up. They may use several different programming languages, depending on what they want to do and what device the player will use. Python, Flash, Assembly, C++, and Java are some languages used.

Game coders work in the following areas:

⇨ **Lead programmers** assign work and maintain schedules. They are skilled coders but spend a lot of time supervising other programmers.

⇨ **Game engine programmers** design the foundation code that the game runs on. This can include developing graphics and designing the physics of the game's engine. These programmers often use low-level languages, so their programs run faster and more efficiently. These programmers have highly technical skills.

⇨ **Artificial intelligence programmers** decide how allies and opponents will react to each of the player's actions. They work to make sure each character's response is realistic.

⇨ **Graphics programmers** create the tools that allow the game's artists to bring their work to the screen. They use advanced math skills to write algorithms that create 2-D and 3-D graphics. These programmers work closely with the artists.

⇨ **Network programmers** write the code that allows players to play online, against or with players around the world. They focus on internet security and ways to prevent cheating.

⇨ **Physics programmers** write the code that defines how objects behave in each game. They aren't bound by the natural laws of physics on earth but by the laws of physics created by the game's designers. For example, how high can a character jump in this world? How far will a car slide on an icy road? What happens when two objects collide?

⇨ **Tools programmers** write the code that automates tasks like creating new levels in the game or importing graphics. They may also craft a game's difficulty levels—not just how characters win or lose, but how they barely win or lose in unusual ways.

⇨ **User interface programmers** write the code that defines a game's menus and create the pop-up displays of important information that a player sees while staying focused on playing the game.

As a video game coder, you must have a bachelor's degree in computer science or computer engineering. You may find a college that has a degree in video game programming, but it's not required. To work in this field, know the programming languages, especially C or C++, understand operating systems, and understand high-level math.

Tips to Succeed as a Video Game Coder

⇨ Play video games. Watch for popular trends and advancements in game technology.

⇨ Think of ways to improve the gaming experience.

⇨ Join a game club in your school or community. If there isn't one, start one!

⇨ Make sure you find and participate in as many internships as possible while in school.

⇨ When you're ready for college, watch for cooperative (co-op) education opportunities with local companies. These are full-time jobs where the student works one term and goes to school the next term, culminating in a degree that takes five to six years to complete.

⇨ Be willing to work for smaller companies as a game programmer. That experience can lead to a better position later on.

⇨ Develop a game. Each one you create can add to your portfolio and help you stand out from the other job applicants.

⇨ Learn how to be a team player.

<Artists/>

Artists design what the game looks like. They create all the artwork for the environment, the characters, and all the objects in the game. They may also design the game's packaging and the game manual. Game artists may use sculptures, pencil drawings, or other means to illustrate their visions for the computer-generated artwork. Digital artists may use 3-D modeling software and motion-capture technology. Animators create models and define the movement of characters and objects.

<Audio Workers/>

Audio workers develop, record, and process all the sounds in a game. This includes music, dialogue, and other sounds, like water running, swords clashing, birds chirping, or a tower falling to the ground. Audio workers include audio designers, engineers, and programmers as well as composers and musicians.

Name: Roxanne Dunn
Job: Lead web developer, A-VIBE Web Development

When did you first become interested in writing computer code and decide to make it the focus of your career?
I became interested in writing code during the summer before I began my first year of college. I attended a summer engineering program called the Stanford Summer Engineering Academy (SSEA). At this program, I was able to take physics, computer science, and other engineering preview classes for a month. I was amazed by the computer science class. I had never heard of computer science before and was fascinated by the possibilities. There is so much that can be achieved through code. I didn't know yet what I wanted to do with my new computer science knowledge, but I knew I wanted to take more computer science classes.

What education/work path did you take to get to your current position?
I have always loved math, so I planned on majoring in math in college, but after the SSEA program, I fell in love with computer science and wanted to study it while still studying math. I met with an advisor, and he told me about this amazing major that combines the two fields—mathematical and computational science at Stanford University. I took classes during the school year and had summer jobs in computer science when I wasn't in school. During one summer, I worked and studying physics at the Lawrence Berkeley National Lab. I wrote a computer program

that predicted how particles would react in the lab's accelerator. The next summer, I worked at the Stanford Linear Accelerator Center and wrote a program that monitored the temperatures of computers at the lab so that workers could be notified when the computers got too hot. During my last summer as a graduate student, I worked as a web developer for Stanford Law School.

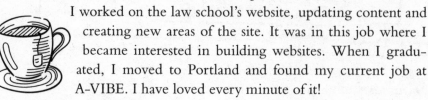

I worked on the law school's website, updating content and creating new areas of the site. It was in this job where I became interested in building websites. When I graduated, I moved to Portland and found my current job at A-VIBE. I have loved every minute of it!

Explain the process you go through to develop a website.
The first steps to building a website involve requirements gathering. This means that we meet with the person or people who want a website, and we learn about them and their website's purpose. We create an outline of the website and then design the website. We determine what the website will look like and what each page will do. When these pieces are decided, then we break up the website project into smaller tasks. Each team member is assigned different, smaller tasks, and we work on the website piece by piece. We test every part of the website and then send it to the client to evaluate. They review it and give us feedback. When everything is complete, we launch the website!

What jobs are there for coders in your company, and what are their coding responsibilities?
We currently have web developers, lead web developers, and an information technology (IT) and database specialist. The web developers are responsible for building parts of the website that are assigned to them. This includes fun animation and any database updates. Our IT and database specialist is in charge of monitoring our servers, which is where the websites live.

What does a normal workday look like for you?
On a normal day, I listen to my favorite music at my computer station while building parts of websites that my managers have

assigned to me. I also check in with my coworkers a few times a day so we can exchange information and help if needed.

What do you enjoy most and least about designing and building websites?

My favorite thing about building websites and about programming in general is that you can create anything with code! We have built calendars, registration sites, shopping sites, online motorcycle and scooter courses, and even card games. It is always fun and exciting, and coders are constantly learning new technologies. My least favorite thing about building websites is when our internet service goes down, and we have to wait to build anything!

What do you think makes a great website?

I think that a great website provides information to its users in a clear way and gives users the ability to do things easily and quickly from their computer or mobile device.

What tips do you have for kids who are interested in writing code for the web?

If you want to be a programmer, I highly encourage you to join computer science clubs and participate in summer programs. You can also learn on your own with online tutorials or books so that you can write code for fun! There is an endless world of possibilities as a coder.

01001001001001001001001001001001001001001000

Animation Coders

Imaginary worlds are created by highly skilled coders who use hard science and precise engineering to make monsters move, planets morph, and characters fight. They help make fantasy worlds look and feel real. These skilled coders also write the software that allows animators to do their work.

To work as an animation coder, you will need a bachelor's degree in computer science or a related field. Plan to study 3-D mathematics and take plenty of programming classes, probably in C++, C, or C#. Look for additional coursework in areas like game development, 3-D animation, and interactive media. Employers may also want you to have some knowledge of gaming software.

While creating a movie or a game using high-tech simulation software may be done by an individual, the coders who create that software work in teams. To gain experience, seek out summer internship programs like those offered by DreamWorks or Pixar Animation Studios or make sure your school has active co-op experiences and that they require a senior design project.

2-D and 3-D Animation

To be 2-D, the image has height and width, but no depth, and it is often used for cartoons on television, commercials, and internet advertisements.

To be 3-D, the image has height, width, and depth, and 3-D animation is used for movies like *Frozen* and *Finding Nemo* and for video games. Animators create a 3-D space on the computer, then use virtual "cameras" to decide what parts of this space to "film."

The jobs for animation programmers fall into the same basic categories as game development programmers. However, it would be wise to have a background in 3-D math, which includes linear algebra. Linear algebra is used to define where things are in space:

⇨ Vectors define specific points in space.

⇨ Matrices define how things transform, becoming smaller or larger.

⇨ Quaternions define how things rotate.

⇨ Rays define how things fly through the air and collide with other things.

⇨ Planes define where and into what the rays collide.

Top Ten Computer Animated Movies

1. *Cars*

2. *Finding Nemo*

3. *How to Train Your Dragon*

4. *Monsters, Inc.*

5. *Shrek*

6. *The Incredibles*

7. *The LEGO Movie*

8. *Toy Story 3*

9. *Up*

10. *Wall-E*

<History of Animated Films/>

1908: Emile Cohl debuts the first all-animated film, *Fantasmagorie*, in Paris. It was composed of seven hundred stitched-together drawings and lasted just over a minute. You can see it on YouTube!

1914: Earl Hurd invents the process of celluloid (cel) animation. In this process, artists use individual sheets of thin, transparent plastic called cels to capture a moment of time in a movie. Using one cel at a time, they paint the characters' slowly changing movements. Each cel is then placed on a painted background and photographed by a movie camera. When the film is played back on a movie projector, the characters appear to be in motion. This process takes a huge amount of time and effort.

1937: Disney's *Snow White and the Seven Dwarves* premieres. It is the first feature-length animated movie. The film took between 570 and 750 crew members almost five years to create.

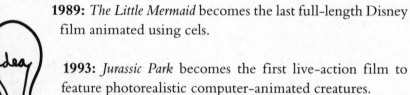

1973: The film *Westworld* uses the first computer-generated images in a brief shot.

1982: Computer-generated images (CGI) are used extensively for the first time in the movie *Tron*.

1989: *The Little Mermaid* becomes the last full-length Disney film animated using cels.

1993: *Jurassic Park* becomes the first live-action film to feature photorealistic computer-animated creatures.

1995: *Toy Story* becomes the first computer-animated film to be released in theaters.

1999: *Star Wars Episode 1: The Phantom Menace* is the first film to use computer-generated imagery extensively for its sets, special effects, and supporting characters.

2004: *The Polar Express* becomes the first fully animated film to use motion-capture technology to render all of its characters.

One of the big challenges for the creators of the movie *Frozen* was that snow had never been convincingly animated. After taking field trips to different snowy and icy places, Disney animators teamed up with UCLA physicists to develop Matterhorn, a snow-simulating algorithm that helped make the snow seem realistic. Coders also created dozens of other tools for this movie, including one that helped sculpt characters' hair, and another that rendered the stretchiness of different fabrics in the characters' clothing. Animating the shot where Elsa builds her ice castle took over four thousand computers thirty hours to render each frame.

Quiz
Design Your Own Game

Before you start coding a video game, you've got to come up with a really great idea. In this activity, you will brainstorm ideas and start building your own game. I've included two different game ideas that you can use as examples.

You will need:

Lots of notecards

A pen or pencil

There are five elements that every game must have: space, goals, components, mechanics, and rules. You will create these elements for your game by listing them on separate notecards. Remember, you won't use every idea that you come up with, but list them all because you never know how one idea might lead to another. Need help? Brainstorming with a partner can be more fun than going it alone and lead to more and possibly better ideas. Grab a friend and start creating!

Space: The world that your game operates within is called the space. This can look very similar to the real world or very different. Space includes the landscape of a game. It also includes the boundaries and barriers, colors, sounds, and lighting.

Example: Tropical Island. This game begins when three companions become stranded on an island. First, we build a map of the island. The island is in the tropics, with a junglelike center surrounded by beaches and then the ocean. The island is fairly large, and there is a mountain on it. There are caves in the mountain. There is only one source of freshwater, located in the heart of the jungle. The ocean serves as a barrier. For colors, there are a lot of greens, blues, and browns. On the beach, there are ocean sounds. Within the jungle, there are sounds of wild animals and wind blowing through the trees. This game takes place during the day and night, so the lighting will change accordingly.

On notecards, we would write the following ideas, each on its own card:

1. Tropical island: sandy beaches surrounding a jungle, with a mountain in the center

2. Freshwater pond located in the center of the jungle

3. Caves in the mountain (here, we would map those out)

4. Barriers: ocean surrounding the island; cliffs on the mountain form challenges

5. Sounds: chirping birds; croaking frogs; rustle of leaves, ocean waves

6. Colors and lighting: blues, greens, and browns; the game changes from day to night, so lighting will change accordingly

You try! What type of world do you want your video game to take place in? You can start with something simple or make your game more complex like the Tropical Island game. What barriers will you create, and how will they look? What colors will you use to give the game the feel you want? What sounds and lighting will you need? Write each element of space on a separate notecard and place them in a stack.

Goals: How will someone win your game? This needs to be specific. Can more than one person win at the game? Are there points, or is there a timer they have to beat? How do they earn these points? Is there only one way to win?

Example—_Tropical Island:_ There are a series of challenges a player must complete before his or her character is rescued. The character has to find freshwater, build a shelter, and build a fire. Finding freshwater would be the easiest—the player must simply explore the island. To build a shelter, however, the player must either find an empty cave or use materials they find to construct a hut. Building fire would require them to find tinder and kindling on the island. Other characters could help with showing how to light the fire, but the player must do it himself or herself.

On notecards, we would write the following ideas, each on its own card:

1. Find freshwater by following animal paths through the jungle.

2. Take freshwater back to your companions in a water bottle.

3. Build a shelter out of fronds and rope.

4. Find a cave that doesn't have an animal in residence, avoiding rats that can eat you!

5. Find materials to build a fire to signal rescuers.

6. Keep companions alive—if you don't bring them water within the time limit, they die, and you lose the game.

You try! How will players win your game? Think about the space you created. What sort of challenges make sense within that space? What is the end goal—do the characters need to defeat a monster?

If so, how do they do that? Do they need to learn a new skill? How will they learn that skill, and who will teach them? Write down all these ideas on notecards. Remember, you don't have to use all the ideas you come up with, but it's a good idea to write them down in case they spark other ideas later on.

Components: Characters, tools, vehicles, food, good guys, bad guys—these are all components, along with any other object in the game. Make sure every component has a purpose—you don't want to spend time coding something that doesn't add any value to your game!

Example—*Tropical Island:* There are three characters. There is the player character named Kris, and two others, Carl and Jessica, who were already stranded on the island when Kris arrived. These other characters will be there to give advice, so the player doesn't get lost.

There are other components as well—a water bottle that can be used to carry water, rope and fronds for building a shelter, fruit that helps Kris reenergize, wild animals he/she must fight when encountering them, and rocks that will help build a fire. See how complicated a game gets when you add interesting things to it? We need to define the animals, the rocks, and everything else that our player needs for the journey.

On notecards, we would write the following ideas, each on its own card:

1. Characters: Kris, Carl, and Jessica with Kris as the main character. Carl and Jessica give advice when needed.

2. Materials: rope and fronds for the shelter; water bottle to carry water; rocks and tinder for the fire; fruit to help Kris reenergize

3. Enemies: wild animals

You try! What are the components in your game? Start with the main character. Then think of what obstacles he or she will face. Do you need to create a villain? A character who gives hints? Signs pointing the way? Will the character be hurt and need a way to replenish his or her strength? Does the character need to gather food, weapons, or magical artifacts along the way? How do your characters get around—a horse, a car, a spaceship? These are all components.

Mechanics: No, these aren't people who fix the cars in your game! Mechanics are the actions of the characters and components. They are the attack moves and weaknesses of characters, the places a vehicle can and can't go, the doors that open when you approach and the ones you have to find a key for. Every component you listed in the last section will have at least one mechanic.

Example—*Tropical Island:* Being able to pick fronds for a shelter is a mechanic. What plants can Kris pick? What plants will hurt it touched? If Kris can swim, this is also a mechanic. However, since the space we have designed is entirely on land, it wouldn't make sense for Kris to swim. If we want Kris to swim, we must first rethink the space and goals in order to make that a useful skill.

On notecards, we would write the following ideas, each on its own card:

1. Kris moves around the island to complete the tasks. He/she can reach up to break off branches to fight off animals, bend down to pick up objects, and kneel down to drink water. He/she can build a fire once Jessica explains how.

2. Carl and Jessica stay near their arrival site. Carl suggests Kris go find water by following an animal trail. Jessica suggests Kris build a shelter and, later, a fire. They need water to survive, so Kris must bring them water or lose the game.

3. The rope and fronds, once assembled into a shelter, can keep wild animals and storms out.

4. Certain fruits will reenergize Kris, but other fruits will take away energy.

You try! Go back to your list of components. List the mechanics that govern each one of them. Do you have a character who goes on a quest? Does that character have a way to attack or defend? Can he or she fly, drive, or dig? These are mechanics for your character. If you have a vehicle, figure out how fast the vehicle goes and where it can go. Are there mountains in your space that are too steep for it to climb? Will it explode if it runs into a rock—or will the rock simply crumble?

Rules: Every game has rules that guide the player, defining how to win the game and what is and isn't allowed.

Example—*Tropical Island:* On notecards, we would write the following ideas, each on its own card:

1. Kris must bring water back to his companions within a time limit before doing any other task.

2. Kris must build a shelter after finding water.

3. Kris must build a fire on the beach to signal rescuers.

4. If Kris fails to bring his/her companions water and food within the time limit, they die, and the game is over.

You try! What rules govern your game? Is there a time limit the player must beat? What happens if the player doesn't make the time—does he or she have to restart? From where? Are there save points? What characters can the player speak to?

As you can see, coming up with a plan for a video game takes a lot of thought. But by spending some extra time thinking through these details at the beginning, you ensure that your game will be easier to create and more fun to play. Happy game creating!

Website Coders

There are only ten kinds of people in this world: those who know binary, and those who don't.

Whenever you use a browser like Chrome or Internet Explorer to look for information on the internet, you are sent to a website. A website can be a single page with information on it, or it can have multiple pages. Since websites go live or go dead every day, to make an exact count of the number of them is like chasing flies. The last time someone reported on the number, there were 14.3 trillion live web pages, and that number is growing at an amazing speed.

That huge number of web pages poses the question "Who creates all those websites and their pages?" The answer is the people who own the domain name, often with the help of website developers. To help you grasp just how big this job area is, take a look at some of these staggering numbers.[1] And, by the time you read this book, the numbers will be even higher.

http://

⇨ 1193 million domains are registered using .com, .org, .net, .gov, and many more.

⇨ There are over 759 million websites online, with 510 million of them being actively maintained.

Microsoft coders created a new HoloLens headset that is a computer you wear around your face. Instead of using a keyboard, mouse, or touchscreen, the user reaches out and touches 3-D images that are projected in front of them. This is still in production, but how cool is that coding? For now, hardcore gamers can get Facebook's virtual reality headset, the Oculus Rift. It requires a PC with tons of computing power and a powerful graphics card. But in the near future, virtual reality coders will blow everyone's minds with the games they create.

⇨ These sites hold over 672 exabytes (EB), or 672,000,000,000 gigabytes (GB), of easily reached data.

⇨ And, over one yottabyte (YB) of stored data. One YB is equal to 1,000,000,000,000,000,000,000,000 bytes!

And who's looking and using all this information?

⇨ Three billion of the world's 6.8 billion people have access to the internet at home.

⇨ There are over 4.3 billion active internet users in the world.

⇨ Of those users, 40 percent access the internet using a computer, 20 percent use a tablet or notebook, and 40 percent use a mobile phone or other mobile device.

⇨ Twitter has about 271 million active users who create five hundred million tweets a day.

⇨ Over 293 billion emails are sent each day, about 204 million each minute worldwide.

⇨ By 2020, there will be more than fifty billion "things" connected to the internet.

Game Jams

Game jams happen when game developers gather together to create a game in a short amount of time. Jams can be local or worldwide events. They can last from one to three days, usually over a weekend, and the games created must adhere to a designated theme. People join in from all areas of the gaming community, including designers, artists, and musicians.

The largest game jam is Global Game Jam. It was first held in 2008. Each site registers for the event. Once the theme is announced, participant teams have exactly forty-eight hours to complete their games. In 2015, the jam was hosted at 518 sites in seventy-eight countries. Teams, made from over twenty-eight thousand registered participants, created over 5,438 games!

How big is the web? Because of its size and the huge amount of information placed on it each day, experts are starting to think of the web as infinite! Even estimating the size of the web to the closest one hundred million pages is becoming an impossible task.

Name: Chris Kite
Job: President and founder, Code 9 Media, Inc.

When did you first become interested in writing computer code and decide to make it the focus of your career?
I received a bachelor's degree from Quincy University in marketing and planned to work in marketing and sales after college.

However, I had a great opportunity to interview with AT&T in their information technology (IT) department as a support analyst. I was fortunate to get the job helping to solve problems users had with their sales and ordering software. At the time, I had very few technical skills or experience. My ability to resolve bug issues in the software was limited to passing emails back and forth between those in development and the end users. I didn't actually fix anything, but I was amazed by those who could! I was drawn to how the developers would pull up a window full of very bizarre characters I couldn't understand, and with a few keystrokes, the problem was solved. I knew at that point, I had found my calling.

What education/work path did you take to get where you are today?
I took a very long path to get where I am today. It was one that was driven by ambition once I realized what I wanted to be in life. In college, I knew I wanted to eventually own my own business. I wasn't sure what that meant, what the business would be, or how I would get there, so I chose to pursue a degree in business. The marketing side of business appealed to me most because it focused on how to sell products and drive growth in a business.

I didn't realize at the time that once college ended, my true education began. At AT&T, I quickly realized I needed to hone my technical skills in order to move into the jobs I desired within the company. So I chose to go back to school and get a master's degree in computer information technology. While I pursued my degree, I also studied a lot of other books to find the answers to things my master's degree would not be able to provide. This was before I realized how powerful a tool the internet would be for me to gain additional skills. As time passed, I was able to obtain development positions within AT&T as well as start my own business. This was due to the skills I learned on the job, my master's degree classes, and using tools such as Google to search for answers to problems I could not solve on my own.

Describe the kind of programming work you do.

The work I currently do is primarily web development and database design. These are the skills used to build the web pages you see when you visit anywhere on the internet. There are many languages used to create web pages, but I focus on a few that help me do my job. They are PHP, JavaScript, SQL, CSS, and HTML. In addition, mobile web development and mobile app development is very popular. This requires a slightly different skill set to create the apps you see on your mobile devices. It's true that all programming languages are different, but once you learn the basics of programming, it allows you to learn other languages more quickly. I remember my first days at AT&T. I felt so intimidated by a screen full of code because I couldn't tell where it started or where it ended. But with time and patience, it began to make sense.

You have a website, Codeconquest.com. Why did you decide to build this site, and what are your goals for it?

I actually own many websites, with Codeconquest.com being a site that focuses on teaching beginners how to code. I learned so much for free from the internet and other free resources that I felt creating a resource that continues this philosophy, as well as expands on it, was a great opportunity to help people find their way.

Codeconquest.com makes up one piece of my overall business. Students of all ages need to realize a website, an app, a piece of software can all be treated like a traditional business you see on the side of the street. Only this business can reach anyone in the world, twenty-four hours a day, seven days a week, 365 days a year.

Over the next five years, there will be a massive need for our youth to learn and understand internet skills because of how much of our technology and daily life is connected through this powerful network. Our schools don't currently teach these skills, which include internet marketing, web development, internet entrepreneurship, as well as others. I feel Codeconquest.com fills a gap.

What do you enjoy most and least about writing code?

The most satisfying part of coding is building all of the individual pieces that will eventually work together to solve a problem or provide value to someone. Creating each software component and plugging those components into each other to build a usable product is very rewarding to me. In addition, there is no one way to write a piece of code. There are many ways to solve the same problem. I like being able to try different approaches and knowing that if I don't like it, I can always change it down the road to make it better—or in some cases, worse.

The part I least enjoy about writing code is trying to understand someone else's code and then having to modify it. As I previously mentioned, there is more than one way to solve a problem, and sometimes another developer wants to solve their problem in the most confusing way possible.

What do you see in the future for computer programming and/or for programmers?

With so many tools (like drag-and-drop development tools and readily available scripts and templates) for the masses to take the difficulty out of development, there will be a rising need for traditional developers to create these tools. There is a lot of complexity in a tool that takes a difficult job and makes it easy for someone less skilled to perform. Overall, I see development and related careers as a high-growth area for many years to come.

What advice would you give to a young person who is interested in becoming a programmer?

My advice is don't be afraid or intimidated by the initial learning curve. I have two *P*'s that I attribute my success to. They are patience and passion. When learning how to code or run your own business, there are so many things to learn. It will be frustrating. You'll want to quit. But you must find the patience to continue. Where does that patience come from? Passion. Your passion will drive you to come back and ultimately acquire the knowledge you need to get the job done. Patience and passion are two very powerful traits that can overcome many other weaknesses.

There are so many resources available to help you get started. Take advantage of these and see if coding is something you want to pursue! Instead of spending fifty dollars on a video game, you can buy a domain name and hosting for a year and create something wonderful!

0100100100100100100100100100100100100010

<Surface Web and Deep Web/>

The part of the internet that you can access using a search engine like Google or Mozilla Firefox is called the surface web. Search engines use software to crawl along the surface of each web page, jumping from link to link, gathering information that is easily accessible. That information is indexed and made available to anyone who is conducting a search. The surface web is what you see and use every day when you search for something online.

There is a large part of the internet, possibly five hundred times the size of the surface web, that isn't accessible by using a search engine. It is called the deep web. This is content that is buried deeper inside sites, hidden behind web search boxes or in areas where you need to type in a query to find it.

For example, let's say you want to learn to write code. You go to Google and type, *Learn to write code*, in the search box. What pops up? A list of companies willing to teach you how to write code and a bunch of articles about writing code. That's what is found on the surface web. The information is great, but none of it actually helps you learn to write code.

Next, you click on one of the sites. Let's say CodeHS.com. Once there, you have to sign up to gain access to the tutorials that will help you learn to write code. That information, all the stuff you get to see once you sign in, is what makes up the deep web. Most of the information found on the deep web is harmless, but some is not. Whenever you search on the web, be cautious and never give out personal information about yourself or your family unless a responsible adult says it's okay.

MIT has designed a programming language called Scratch to help young kids learn the basics of coding a video game. Using code that is written and bundled into blocks, they snap together programs much like you snap together LEGOs. The blocks allow the coders to create games or stories or animate anything they can imagine from dogs jumping to elephants swinging their trunks. Children in over 150 countries who speak more than forty different languages play with Scratch and have shared over nine million projects online.

\<Careers Coding for the Web/\>

Web developers meet with clients who need websites designed. They listen to their needs and then design websites that will function for them. They can make artistically pleasing websites but don't necessarily have the coding expertise to make them function properly. Some web developers write the code that builds a website, but often this job is passed on to a front-end programmer.

Front-end/client-side developers write code that defines what people see when they open web pages. Besides having some design skills, they should know how to write in HTML, which is the backbone of all web applications; cascading style sheets (CSS), which sets the rules for the layout of the page; and JavaScript, which is used for functions and interactivity on the pages. These coders make sure that a site is correctly seen in all browsers and on every device. They make sure the site is well organized and users can find important information quickly. And they make sure the site loads and opens as quickly as possible.

Back-end/server-side developers write code that manages websites behind the scenes. They build the structures on which the front-end developer works. They work with the server that hosts a website; the applications used on the site, like those that display items or complete purchases; and the database that stores all the information. Website security is very important and on every back-end developer's list of responsibilities. Having an understanding of how to keep information safe is essential to excelling in this career. Back-end developers often write using languages like PHP, Ruby, Python, Java, or C++.

Konami Code

Kazuhisa Hashimoto created the Konami Code in 1986 while working on an arcade game. He thought the game was too hard, so he created a cheat code to give a player more power quickly. The code wasn't removed when the game was released, and other players found it. The code was included in sequels to the game. The Konami Code is ↑ ↑ ↓ ↓ ← → ← → BA. This sequence can vary depending on the button layout of the video game console.

The Konami Code has become a popular method for unlocking bonus features on popular websites. For example, in 2009, a coder added glittery unicorns and rainbow graphics that could be seen on ESPN.com. In 2010, a coder changed the headlines on Newsweek.com to say, if someone entered the code, that there was a zombie invasion.

Full-stack developers work in two areas. They work on the back end of web programming but are able to transition to the front end with an understanding of design and functionality. A coder with this level of technical skill is rare because it requires a vast amount of knowledge and skill. Full-stack developers should understand how every level of the web works.

Whichever area interests you, it is important that you know how to pay attention to detail, are able to learn quickly, can solve problems, and can communicate well with other people.

<The Internet Timeline/>

1961: Leonard Kleinrock publishes a paper titled "Information Flow in Large Communication Nets." The idea of the internet is born.

1962: J. C. R. Licklider pushes the idea of a "galactic network." Robert Taylor joins in to help create ARPANET, a network of computers that would later become known as the internet.

1965: The first dial-up connection between two computers, one in Massachusetts and one in California, happens.

1968: The Network Working Group (NWG) holds its first meeting to discuss ways to get computer servers to talk to each other. In December, the final version of the specifications for the Interface Message Processor (IMP) was written.

1969: On July 3, a University of California, Los Angeles, press release tells the public about the internet. In October, the first internet message is sent. The first attempt failed and is considered the first network crash. The second attempt worked.

1971: Ray Tomlinson sends the first email message.

1973: Yogen Dalal and Carl Sunshine help design Trans-mission Control Protocol (TCP) and internet protocol (IP). TCP/IP becomes the language that governs communication for all computers on the internet.

1974: ARPANET becomes the first internet service provider (ISP).

1977: Although the modem was first released in 1960, this is the year when Dale Heatherington and Dennis Hayes released their 80-103A modem, the first designed for the personal computer. It connected to any phone and had a price that meant anyone who wanted to could get online.

1978: Gary Thuerk sends the first spam email.

1979: The first commercial online service, CompuServe, uses a dial-up connection and is available to everyone.

1984: The domain name system is introduced. Symbolics.com is the first internet domain name. A Massachusetts computer company registered it in 1985.

1989: The World, headquartered in Brookline, Massachusetts, becomes the first US commercial dial-up ISP.

1990: A Swiss programmer named Tim Berners-Lee develops HTML, the language that defines how the internet is viewed and navigated.

1991: Berners-Lee introduces the World Wide Web (WWW), a series of sites and pages that are connected using links. WWW is what made the internet the popular and useful tool that it is today.

1995: The dot-com boom starts as large companies and individuals create web pages to make money.

1996: Sergey Brin and Larry Page develop a way to search the web and call it Google.

1999: Kevin Ashton coins the term *Internet of Things* and establishes MIT's Auto-ID Center, a global network of academic research laboratories.

2000: The dot-com bust happens when many online companies fail. LG announces the first internet-connected refrigerator.

Six Popular Animation Software Packages

1. Toon Boom Studio 8 is storyboarding and animation software, primarily for 2-D animation. It was used in *The LEGO Movie*.

2. Autodesk's 3ds MAX is used for 3-D modeling, animation, and rendering.

3. Adobe Photoshop CS6 is an artist's tool for editing photos and creating original images.

4. MARI is 3-D texture-painting software. DreamWorks used this in *Mr. Peabody and Sherman* and *How to Train Your Dragon 2*.

5. Unity Pro 4 gives you the tools needed to create games that will work with more than one operating system—on Linux, Android, and Apple devices. More games are made with Unity than any other game engine. To use Unity you will need to know a programming language like JavaScript, C#, or Boo.

6. Blender is open source, 3-D animation software. It was one of the tools used for the movie *Big Hero 6*.

2005: The United Nations recognizes the Internet of Things.

2008: The first international Internet of Things conference is held in Zurich, Switzerland.

2010: Google introduces its self-driving vehicle project, the beginning of the internet-connected, driverless car.

2010: Bluetooth Low Energy (BLE) is introduced. It leads the way in networking applications used in the fitness, healthcare, security, and home entertainment industries.

2011: IPv6 is launched. This protocol increases the number of "things" that can connect to the internet by increasing the number of IP addresses by 340 undecillion. That number is 1 followed by thirty-six zeros!

2014: Cisco Systems, a worldwide leader in networking, estimates that 12.1 billion internet-connected devices are in use this year. They predict that number will be over fifty billion by 2020.

 # \<Spotlight/\>

William Henry "Bill" Gates III (b. 1955), Founder of Microsoft, World's Largest Software Company

Bill Gates was born on October 28, 1955, in Seattle, Washington. His father was a lawyer and his mother was a stay-at-home mom who spent her free time working on community and charity projects. Gates, along with his two sisters, was raised to be competitive and encouraged to excel in activities.

When Gates was thirteen, his parents recognized that he was bored in school. To keep him from becoming too withdrawn, they transferred him to Lakeside School, a school with a very challenging curriculum. Gates thrived in the new environment, excelling in every subject, from math to drama.

At Lakeside, Gates met Paul Allen, a boy who would become his good friend and future business partner. The two bonded over their love of computers and spent most of their free time figuring out what a computer could do and writing programs in BASIC. Gates wrote a player vs. computer tic-tac-toe game, and together they wrote a payroll program for a computer company and a class-scheduling program for their school.

In 1970, when Gates was fifteen and Allen was seventeen, they started their own business. Their first project was a program that monitored traffic patterns, and they sold it for $20,000. The two wanted to continue working together, but Gates's parents insisted that he go on to college, hoping he would follow in his father's footsteps and become a lawyer.

With excellent high school grades and a 1590 out of 1600 on his SAT test, Gates was admitted into Harvard University in 1973. However, he wasn't very interested in his studies and spent most of his time in the computer lab. One day, Allen showed Gates an article about the Altair 8800 mini-computer kit. The two were fascinated by the idea of personal computers and the possibility of writing software to run on them.

Without touching one of the computers, Gates and Allen wrote a software program for the Altair 8800. When the program was finished, Allen traveled to Albuquerque, New Mexico, to demonstrate it to the president of Micro Instrumentation and Telemetry Systems (MITS). The software worked! Allen was quickly hired on at MITS, and much to his parents' dismay, Gates left Harvard to work with him.

It wasn't long before Gates and Allen became partners again and started a new company they called Microsoft, a name that came from the blending of the words *microcomputer* and *software*. In 1978, Gates moved Microsoft's headquarters to Bellevue, Washington, where he and Allen continued to write software in different formats for different computer companies. At this point, Microsoft had twenty-five employees and gross sales of $2.5 million. At the age of twenty-three, Gates was the head of the company, its lead software developer, and the company's spokesman.

In 1980, computer giant IBM was looking for someone to write software for their new personal computer. They contacted Microsoft, and Gates promised to produce the software. However, there was one problem. He didn't have access to IBM's operating system. Without telling IBM, he bought an operating system that ran on computers similar to IBM's and adapted the software to run on the IBM PC. IBM wanted to buy the software's source code, but Gates refused. Microsoft retained the rights and only licensed the program to IBM. This was a genius business move, and by the end of 1981, Microsoft had 128 employees and sales of $16 million.

Allen resigned from Microsoft in 1984, and under Gates's leadership, the company grew quickly. The next big innovation for Gates was the Windows operating system. It would be compatible with the keyboard and text MS_DOS system but was more user-friendly. With a Windows operating system, a computer user would see graphics instead of text on the screen and use a mouse rather than the keyboard to navigate.

In 1994, Gates married Melinda French. The couple has three children, Jennifer, Rory, and Phoebe. Over the years, Microsoft has released many popular software programs including Microsoft Office and Microsoft Internet Explorer. When Gates took Microsoft public in 1986, he became a millionaire and, within a year, a billionaire. Today, he is worth around $79 billion and is one of the richest men in the world.

Gates stepped down as CEO in 2000 to focus on software development. Then in 2006, he announced that he was leaving Microsoft to pursue his charity work. His last full day of work at Microsoft was June 27, 2008.

Over the years, Gates and his wife have spent much of their time and money supporting education and world health and improving impoverished communities through their private nonprofit foundation, the Bill and Melinda Gates Foundation.

Name: Jake Galant
Age: 18
Job (when not studying!): Director, TeraByte Video Game Creation Camp

When did you first discover that you were interested in writing code?

When I was six years old, I attended my brother's first video game design camp and fell in love with designing my own games. Every year after that first year, I moved on to making more detailed and advanced games and learned new techniques.

How did you get started at TeraByte Video Game Creation Camp?

TeraByte Video Game Creation Camp was started by my brother, Zach, when he was in the ninth grade. For the first two years, Zach rented a computer lab at his school. Then he bought computers and created a computer lab in our garage. Over the past twelve years, several hundred paying students have come to camp to learn the basics of video game design.

I started out as a camper. Then I became a counselor-in-training and eventually a full-time counselor. When I was in the eighth grade, I took over as camp director, since Zach was off at college and working other places during the summers. Ever since, I have run the whole camp, including sales, teaching classes, and designing curriculum; hiring, training, and supervising counselors; setup, recess games, technical problem solving, and dealing with parents.

What is Tera Byte Outreach and what are your goals for it?
Tera Byte Outreach is a separate division of TeraByte that I started that aims to provide video game design instruction to underprivileged kids around Dallas and around the world. The first summer, I started the program at one school for about fifteen students. The program has grown over the past four years, and this summer includes five schools with about 120 students. I now have twelve volunteer counselors/teachers and run three sessions simultaneously, each of two weeks, in June. In four years of the program, I have taught 270 kids in Dallas, China, and Israel.

I use the profits from the camp to provide the program, snacks, certificates, culmination party, and T-shirts to the outreach camp students. My goal for the program is to provide this education for as many underprivileged kids as possible. This is why I also created an online course where I recorded ten videos, each teaching one lesson of the program. I share these programs with schools, so their students can watch the videos and then create and share their games with me via Dropbox. I can see their games and answer their questions remotely.

The most difficult aspects of creating and running TeraByte Outreach are getting to the decision maker—the principal or counselor—and getting that person to reply and make a commitment. For example, this summer, after multiple phone calls and emails went unreturned, I had to go in person four times to meet with the assistant principal at one school, even though it was the third year we were running the camp there. The good news is that she ended up wanting two weeks instead of one, so I got a bonus for that effort. At other times, a principal will tell me that she wants the camp, but then she does not make it happen because she does not get the district permission she thinks she needs. Recently, I was able to get another school to sign up because I offered to bring their kids to a nearby school where we were running another camp. This overcame various authorization, installation, and supervision problems of that new school.

Another challenge is with the installation of the software on each computer. The computers are old, so loading the program takes longer than normal—many hours per school. Unfortunately, the computer teacher in the school's lab does not have control over the district computer technician, so often the computers are wiped clean by the district in between camp one year and the next, and I have to reinstall the program on each computer. I have learned to allow time for this or to make sure the computers are put into deep freeze after installation.

Why are you interested in working with kids and helping them learn to write code?
I have been lucky to have a great education and lots of chances to have extra learning and enrichment like summer science classes, four years on a Destination Imagination Team, Children's International Summer Villages (CISV), early experience at TeraByte with my brother, a Chinese immersion camp for a month, a Stanford summer creative writing camp, debate camps, etc. I know that these experiences are important to my future, and I know that other kids, who cannot afford these camps or whose parents do not even know about these activities, need those experiences and would love them too. Also, I have learned how much coding can help with thinking and problem solving. I have heard my family discussing the importance of creative problem solving for the future of the

United States in the global economy. And I can see how coding is part of almost everything we do and are involved in, so I can see that it is a critical skill for kids to learn and learn from.

And I like teaching. I like explaining things that I know about to help someone else understand them. And the kids are fun—most of the time.

You are studying Chinese and went to China to teach coding. Describe your experiences there.

I organized a Terabyte camp at the Beijing International School. The school lent me space and a computer lab. With the help of an administrator at the school, we were able to invite about fifteen Chinese kids from a local public school to take part in the camp. Two of the kids were also Boy Scouts, so in addition to the regular game design curriculum, I taught them the curriculum for two merit badges: computer and game design. Those two boys spoke English but were raised in China. The program I used is the one I use in the United States and is in English.

I was able to communicate with the Chinese kids because of my study of Mandarin (Chinese). I also studied up on the specific vocabulary that I would need to teach game design. I learned that I could use my classroom Mandarin to communicate in a real-world situation and that the language of programming and game design is pretty universal. I realized how my language study helped me interact with kids in another country and with another culture. I also learned how much we are alike.

How do you balance your schoolwork with all your other activities?

My schoolwork is the most important priority. I do my homework every day so I do not get behind. I try to get some work done during free time at school also. Crew is after school, so I cannot start my homework until about 7:00 PM for about two-thirds of the school year. The hardest part is doing homework when I am traveling for debate tournaments. I always have to miss some school for that as well. I am lucky that my friends take good notes and share them with me. I have to do some work while we are on the plane because we are busy debating, preparing for the debate, or helping other members of our team while we are at the tournament.

Since I run the TeraByte camps during the summer, it does not affect my schoolwork that much. The main TeraByte work during the school year is planning the summer, which includes lining up the schools, counselors, and campers. I have to write emails, make phone calls, and meet with school administrators. I have a very busy summer, but all my activities—debate camp, TeraByte, and Chinese study—are in separate weeks.

Where do you see yourself in ten years?
I think I will probably be in law school. Right now I like the law, public policy, and science and technology. Since I enjoy science and technology, and learned about intellectual property rights two years ago when I focused on it for the "economic engagement with Mexico" debate topic, I may become a patent attorney. But since I like public policy and international issues, I might be in the Foreign Service or work for the State Department.

010010010010010010010010010010010010010010

Artificial Intelligence and Robots

An optimist says, "The glass is half full."
A pessimist says, "The glass is half empty."
A programmer says, "The glass is twice
as large as necessary!"

Artificial intelligence coders fall into two categories, those who work for the gaming industry and those who work in other areas, like telecommunications, the military, or academia. You learned about gaming in a previous chapter, so this is where you'll learn about other careers that use AI programming skills. Although the two career paths often intersect, over time they are becoming very different career choices.

<What Is Artificial Intelligence?/>

AI is the part of computer science that focuses on creating intelligent machines that can work with and react to humans. In a 1950 paper titled "Computing Machinery and Intelligence," Alan Turing, who knows a thing or two about theoretical computer science and artificial intelligence, talked about the possibility of creating a machine

Google's small, egg-shaped prototype has been driving along the streets of Mountain View, California, at a whopping twenty-five miles an hour. According to Google's director of the self-driving project, Chris Urmson, "During this next phase of our project, we'll have safety drivers aboard with a removable steering wheel, accelerator pedal, and brake pedal that allow them to take over driving if needed."[1] Google has already tested vehicles equipped with self-driving technology. Tesla Motors and Mercedes-Benz also have self-driving cars in their future plans.

that could mimic a human being. His paper opens with the words, "I propose to consider the question, 'Can machines think?'"[2]

He proposed a test, called the Imitation Game, to verify a computer's ability to think like a human. In his test, now known as the Turing Test, a person is put at one terminal and a computer at another. A judge, seated in another room, types questions into his terminal and the two contestants respond. The judge must then decide which respondent is human and which is machine. If the judge is correct less than 50 percent of the time, the machine can be considered intelligent. The game is also played where there is only one contestant, and the judge must decide if it is human or a machine.

Around the world, research institutions and universities are working on artificial intelligence. If the idea of creating a machine that thinks like a person is interesting to you, this might be a great area of computer coding to pursue.

AI programmers work at the following tasks:

⇨ Writing speech-recognition software like that used on most smartphones, handwriting software that students use to take notes, and face- and object-recognition software used by law enforcement and the military

➡ Teaching machines to think like humans

➡ Working with robotics, which requires the machine be intelligent enough to navigate around, perform tasks, and manipulate objects

➡ Creating games where humans play against a machine like in video games or chess matches

➡ Working with financial institutions that use AI for investing and for keeping track of their properties

➡ Helping medical centers and hospitals where they use AI for scheduling appointments, accessing medical records, and processing medical images to look for abnormalities

➡ Working in industry, where AI is used in robots that perform tasks that are too dangerous for people to do, like handling bombs, or tasks that are repetitive but vital and where a mistake could cost lives

➡ Updating automated online assistance or telephone call centers with speech-recognition software to interact with humans and perform basic but limited tasks

➡ Creating smart toys like the Furby and Drive, where AI allows them to speak and act

➡ Making what seems like magic in the music industry, where AI software is programmed to mimic musicians or singers

➡ Supporting the military and airline industries with AI for combat and flight simulations, as well as object recognition

➡ Helping the Office of Homeland Security use AI to gather a lot of data and to filter out email spam

The History of Smart Toys

Automation was first mentioned in ancient Chinese writings, Jewish legends, and Greek myths, but the first known clockwork mechanism is the Antikythera mechanism. It dates to the first century BCE and was used for calculating the position of the stars.

The first mechanism that could be considered a "toy" is at the Smithsonian. It is a clockwork monk that stands about fifteen inches (380 mm) tall and dates to around 1560 CE. When the monk is wound up, he walks in a square path, pounding his chest with his right arm. He also raises and lowers his left hand while holding a wooden cross and a rosary, turns and nods his head, rolls his eyes, and mouths silent funeral prayers. The monk even occasionally brings the cross to his lips and kisses it!

Over the next several centuries, there were cuckoo clocks, music boxes, and then automated mechanical toys. In the late 1900s, toys started to have media players inside and used a pull string to make them talk, like the Chatty Cathy doll.

When the microprocessor came along in the mid-1970s, true smart toys began to appear on the market. There were educational toys like Speak & Spell and the robotic teddy bear Teddy Ruxpin that could tell stories while moving its mouth and eyes.

Today, smart toys use speech recognition to understand and respond to the words the child is saying. They start with a list of known words and then learn more as the child teaches them. A popular smart toy is LEGO Mindstorms. Using LEGOs along with sensors and processors, kids can create and control their own robots.

\<AI Programming Languages/>

⇨ IPL (which was the first AI programming language)

⇨ C++

⇨ Haskell

⇨ Lisp

⇨ Planner

⇨ POP-11

⇨ Prolog

⇨ STRIPS

Name: Ethan Schaezler
Age: 16
Job (when not studying!): Robot Coder

When did you first discover that you were interested in writing code?
I have been interested in technology and science, and intrigued by computers, since I was very young. In 2006, I got a Mac Mini (for sharing with my brother), and I began to get even more interested in the world of computers. With that computer, I did an assortment of more advanced things such as audio and video editing and compilation. In 2009, after getting a Samsung NC10 Netbook, primarily for word processing initially, I began getting a more diverse experience of what is available in the world of computers.

A notable turning point in my use of computers was when I heard of Linux, which was different from the familiar Windows or Mac OS operating systems, and was even available for free! The distro [distribution] that I started out with was Ubuntu Linux version 9.04. I started running it off of a live CD until I eventually installed it in a dual-boot configuration with Windows XP. Quite a substantial amount of the system was more accessible and apparent than it was in Windows and Mac OS X, and I began to look into more advanced things to do on computers.

While in elementary school, the option of doing FLL (First LEGO League) came up. Since I was already interested in technology, computers, science, and making things, this was an appealing opportunity. For me, one of the most interesting aspects about FLL was the programming aspect. FLL utilized the LEGO NXT, which included the NXT brick, which did all of the computational tasks for the robot. (The robots in FLL are made out of LEGO components only, which included the motors, sensors, and various other peripherals for the NXT.)

For FLL, the NXT is programmed with NXT-G, a graphical LabView-derived programming language made specifically for the NXT. With NXT-G, I was introduced to and familiarized with numerous programming concepts such as loops, conditional statements, etc. Additionally, I learned a substantial amount of things pertaining to the logic that is used for programming robots.

How did you learn to write code, and what language(s) do you know?

I first learned to write code through FLL and by using NXT-G. I later began to work on learning C, using some books on programming it. When I started doing FTC (First Tech Challenge), I was again using NXT bricks, but instead of using NXT-G, a version of C designed for robots called RobotC was being used. Through FTC, I learned quite a bit more about programming with C and programming in general. For this year in FTC, the new platform utilizes Android phones programmed in Java instead of C. Having access to this more powerful platform will be beneficial, but it means that I have to learn Java if I want to program the robot using the new and required platform. I have been learning Java by using a book and by taking a Java class. By having knowledge about programming in C, learning Java has been easier than it was to learn C. It helps that Java is in the C family as well as that it utilizes logic consistent with programming in general.

Tell about some of the programming you have done.
One of the most elaborate and most interesting programs that I have worked on was the code that I used last FTC season to control and operate the robot. One particularly interesting aspect of the code was the utilization of PID (proportional integral derivative) for the synchronization of the speeds of all of the wheels. This was an important element since the robot was using Mecanum wheels, which allow for moving sideways and diagonally, as well as forward and backward, but can have undesired arcing occur with them due to their subjectivity to uneven weight distribution among the wheels. Synchronizing the wheels using PID helped fix the issue of the undesired arcing. This was an instance where having libraries available was incredibly helpful.

Another interesting aspect of the program was the ability to dock with the goals. Part of the challenge was to score points by putting balls into tubes that were upright and movable. These goals had a hexagonal base. The strategy was to attach to the movable goals so that we could then utilize a mechanism consisting of two "rollers" to capture the balls and then fling them up into an adjustable chute, which would then direct them into the goals.

The system that allowed for the docking with the goals involved two "grabbers" and two EOPD (electro-optical proximity detector) sensors. In the code, I implemented two different methods for having the robot dock with the goals automatically. One utilized a function called SimpleDock, which would dock with the goals once the value from one of the EOPD sensors was within a certain range of values and the other sensor had similar values to the first. This function was utilized during teleop, when there is a driver operating the robot, so that the robot could easily dock with the goals. Previously, it was difficult to see if the robot was within the range that was required to dock with the goals successfully.

The second function, called SmartDock, allowed for docking with the goals by actually controlling the robot to move itself toward the goal. This worked by getting the values from both EOPD sensors and then attempting to get both sensors to output a value that fits within a particular range by moving both sides of the robot slightly. If it did not have both EOPD sensors output a value that fit within the range after moving forward a particular distance, it would arc and then move forward again. This made it so that the robot could successfully dock with the goals even if it collided with one of the vertices of the base of a goal.

How did you first become interested in robots and decide to enter competitions?

I began getting involved in For Inspiration and Recognition of Science and Technology (FIRST) robotics in elementary school when an FLL team was being formed. The programming aspect of it particularly appealed to me. In FLL there are two portions—the robotics portion and the project portion. Both portions are themed around a particular real-world challenge. The robot is programmed to operate completely autonomously. The project portion requires that a solution for a particular aspect of the main issue, in which the entire challenge for that year is themed, be made and presented to a panel of judges by the team. I continued doing FLL up into high school. I now do First Tech Challenge (FTC).

What do you do to prepare for a competition?

For FTC, I prepare by generating and testing many ideas that are applicable to FTC in general. Additionally, our team meets, and we discuss our ideas, along with other things like funding and what materials and tools we might need.

Why do you think it's important that your peers learn how to write code?

Everyone interacts with computers pretty much every day. It simply makes sense to know more about them. It also makes complete sense to know programming, since computers are programmed. And computers are tools, and a tool works best when it can be used to its full potential. In nearly every modern job, computers will be used, so having competency with programming is quite relevant.

Programming also encourages logical thinking and troubleshooting, which are skills that are useful everywhere. Additionally, programming is simply fun. It opens up the opportunity to create many interesting projects that require code. If you don't know how to program and understand computers, you run the risk of becoming less in control of the computer and having the computer be more in control of you.

How do you balance your schoolwork with all your other activities?
Robotics and my other assorted coding-related projects can take up a lot of time (especially in addition to orchestra), but I attempt to do my schoolwork before doing my programming and robotics projects. I find it helpful to create a general agenda for when I plan to complete things so that I don't spend too much time on one particular thing.

Where do you see yourself in ten years?
I plan to expand my knowledge of programming and knowledge in general. I plan to continue learning more about computers, science, technology, and the world as a whole.

0100100100100100100100100100100100100010010010010

Robotics Engineers

From the 1960s television cartoon *The Jetsons* and that family's robot maid Rosie, to Hiro and his robot friend, Baymax, in the 2014 movie *Big Hero 6*, robots have fascinated television watchers and moviegoers. There are good robots like Iron Giant and the Autobots that struggle to save their human friends and bad robots like the Decepticons and

Terminator that seek to destroy humanity. From the time robots were first imagined to today, there has been a struggle between robots as a force for good and the possibility that, by creating them, things could go terribly, horribly, awfully wrong.

The reality? We're a long way from creating a machine that can take over the world! Sigh of relief. For now, they can play a great game of chess, drive around the surface of Mars, help the police defuse a bomb, and assemble products in a manufacturing facility.

What do all these robots have in common? Their work can be done using a list of specific, albeit complex, tasks that a coder writes and uploads into their memory.

<What Is a Robot?/>

A robot is a machine that can move its body using a reprogrammable computer as its brain. If you want the robot to do something, you program it. If you want to change what it's doing, you can reprogram it.

Robotics engineers design and maintain robots, develop new ways to use them, and conduct research to push the limits of a robot's abilities. They use computer-aided design and drafting (CADD) and computer-aided manufacturing (CAM) software, but knowing how to write code is important in the creation of job-specific robots.

Here are some examples of areas where you may work if you decide to specialize in coding robots.

1. **Agriculture:** Robots are being used to harvest crops, including fragile fruits and vegetables. The Lettuce Bot is one such robot; it can pick fragile lettuce without damaging it.

2. **Automobiles:** Robots are assembling cars, testing safety equipment, and welding parts.

3. **Construction:** Robots work to cut, stack, bundle, package, and put materials onto pallets. They also weld metal parts, apply adhesives, and assemble doors and windows.

Robot, the Word

The word *robot* came from the Czech word *robota*, or "forced labor." Robot was the name playwright Karel Capek gave to the machines in his 1920 science fiction play, *R.U.R.* The play is about how robots were given human emotions and then turned on their human creators. The robot rebellion led to the extinction of the human race. Although Capek is given credit for coining the word *robot* in his play, in a 1933 article for the Czech newspaper *Lidové noviny*, he reassigned that credit to his brother Josef.

The word *robotics*, used to describe the study and creation of robots, was first used by science fiction writer Isaac Asimov. In his 1942 short story *Runaround*, he defined the Three Laws of Robots. These rules, whether kept or broken, are the source of conflict in many man-versus-machine books and movies.

1. A robot may not injure a human being or, through inaction, allow a human being to come to harm.

2. A robot must obey the orders given it by human beings, except where such orders would conflict with the First Law.

3. A robot must protect its own existence as long as such protection does not conflict with the First or Second Laws.

4. **Entertainment:** Robots are becoming popular toys and pet companions.

5. **Healthcare:** Robots like CosmoBot work with developmentally disabled children. PARO is a robot that can replace a therapy animal. Robots also work with patients, distribute medications, and assist in surgery.

6. **Laboratories:** Robots test new and innovative ideas in universities, engineering companies, and research facilities.

7. **Law Enforcement and the Military:** Robots patrol dangerous areas, defuse bombs, perform surveillance for security, assist in hostage situations, and remove the injured from dangerous situations.

8. **Manufacturing:** Robots take over those jobs that are repetitive, like packing, painting, and assembly. They also do more complex jobs where human error could cause injury or death.

9. **Mining:** Robots do the most dangerous work, digging, exploring, and transporting minerals from areas where it's too dangerous for human workers.

10. **Utility Companies:** Robots run along power lines to detect wear and tear and move through gas and water lines to watch for weak areas that could rupture.

11. **Warehouses:** Robots do most of the repetitive stacking, which eliminates worker injury.

12. **Space Exploration:** Robots work in the vacuum of space, orbit planets, and even walk on Mars. Robonaut is NASA's new space robot that looks and works like a human. It can go where humans cannot.

L33T Profile

Name: Sonia Chernova
Job: Assistant professor, Georgia Institute of Technology

When did you first become interested in writing computer code and decide to make it the focus of your career?
I wasn't a computer whiz as a kid. I knew my way around the computer enough to do my homework, play some games, and

Famous Robots in Industry, Movies, and Television

⇨ AIBO: robotic pets created by Sony that learn through human interaction

⇨ ASIMO: a robot created by Honda that can walk on two legs like a person

⇨ Data: the almost-human android from *Star Trek: The Next Generation*

⇨ HAL: the ship's computer in Stanley Kubrick's *2001: A Space Odyssey*

⇨ Iron Giant: a fifty-foot metal-eating giant robot in *The Iron Giant* movie

⇨ Mars Rover: NASA's robot that was sent to Mars

⇨ R2D2 and C-3PO: the intelligent robots in the *Star Wars* movies

⇨ Robot: the robot in the 1960s television series *Lost in Space*

⇨ Rosie: the robot in the 1960s animated series *The Jetsons*

⇨ Sonny: the robot in the 2004 movie *I, Robot*

⇨ WALL-E: the robot in the 2008 animated film *WALL•E*

chat with friends, but I never understood what it takes to make a computer work. In school, my favorite classes were math and science, but neither seemed like the ideal job for me. As I was finishing high school, my parents encouraged me to try computer science. I tried my first programming class during my senior year of high school. I found it surprisingly easy and fun, so I decided to major in computer science in college.

When did you become interested in robots and decide to focus your coding career on them?

I studied computer science at Carnegie Mellon University in Pittsburgh, which happens to also have one of the world's largest robotics centers, called the Robotics Institute. It was there, while taking the introduction to artificial intelligence course, that I became fascinated with robots.

Robots exist at a meeting point between computer programming and the physical world. Programming robots is very satisfying when it works well because you get to see your code really do something in the real world. And when it doesn't work, your code's errors, called bugs, can make your robot do some crazy (and funny!) things. My first robotics project was to program robot dogs to play soccer in order to study how robots can be designed to work together as a team. It was a great project, and I loved seeing the effects of my code in the real world.

What education/work path did you take to get to your current position?

To become a professor, I first finished college and then completed a PhD, also in computer science. During this time, I had several summer internships in robotics, including a three-month stay in Tokyo, Japan. I also traveled to many robotics conferences to present my work to others working in my field, visiting Italy, Portugal, England, and Germany.

Describe some of the projects you've worked on.

My work focuses on finding ways in which we can program robots to enable them to learn. Traditionally, when we think of robots, we think of machines that do the same task over and over. This is true of robots that work in factories and warehouses where there are many repetitive tasks, but robots working in environments that are less predictable must be able to adapt. For example, consider buying a cleaning robot for your home. Your house is unique in its own way, both because of the things you own and because you like to arrange and do things in your own way. Because of these differences, the company that created the robot has no way to program it with everything it needs to know in order to clean your house *your* way. For example, the robot might be able to recognize grocery items, but just as a friend visiting your house for the first time would not know how to put the items away in all the right places, neither could the robot. Like your friend, the robot also needs to be teachable. Needs to be able to learn.

My work focuses on enabling everyday people to teach robots new skills so that one day you can buy a robot, bring it home, and teach it how you like things to be done simply by showing it around your house. The algorithms we develop are often called learning from demonstration because the goal is to make it possible for the robot to learn by watching the demonstrations made by the human user.

What does an average day look like for you as the director of the Robot Autonomy and Interactive Learning (RAIL) lab?

I spend much of my day discussing projects with my students, getting updates on the latest results, and planning next steps. One of the most exciting things about my job is the freedom to explore the challenges and problems that excite me the most, and we are always discovering something new. I also teach classes in robotics and computer science, meet with visitors, and help review the recent work of others in my field.

What do you see in the future for careers in robotics?

Career options in robotics will grow tremendously in the coming years! Robots are at the cusp of entering the everyday lives of millions of people through advances such as self-driving cars, cleaning robots, and flying delivery drones. Medicine is another tremendous interest area for robotics, with potential applications in prosthetics, autonomous wheelchairs, smart homes, rehabilitation, and surgery. Across all these areas, many jobs will focus on building the robotic systems themselves, while many more will be focused on understanding how robots can be integrated as useful tools into current practices and society at large.

Do you have any tips for kids who are interested in working with robots?

Robotics is more popular than ever, with many middle school and high school clubs starting up in recent years. If you're interested in getting involved, see if your school already offers a club, or help start your own. Also take a look at nationwide programs, such as FIRST [usfirst.org], which often can help direct you to local groups.

0100100100100100100100100100100100100100010

 # \<Spotlight/\>

George Devol (1912–2011), Inventor of the First Programmable Robotic Arm

George Devol was born in Louisville, Kentucky, in 1912. Throughout his early years, he was fascinated with anything mechanical or electrical. He struggled with learning from books but thrived on working with his hands. During his high school years, he helped maintain the school's electric light plant and was always imagining new ways to use vacuum tubes, besides building a radio.

When he was twenty years old, he decided not to go to college but to go into business instead. His new company, United Cinephone, produced a product that recorded sound directly onto film. When he discovered that big companies like RCA and Western Electric were already in the market, he stopped production and steered his company in a different direction.

His next product was a photoelectric switch that could be used to open a door automatically. He licensed the patent to Yale and Towne, and they manufactured automatic doors that sold around the world. For his company, Devol also invented Orthoplane lighting for factories, which was brighter and easier to install, optical controls for offset printing presses, and an early bar code system that Railway Express Company used for sorting packages. And in 1939, his company installed automated photoelectric counters at the entrances to the New York World's Fair and counted each customer who walked through the gates.

During World War II, he sold his interest in his company and went to work for Sperry Gyroscope, developing radar devices and testing microwave equipment. A few years later, he moved on to working with radar devices for the US Navy and Air Force. His radar systems were mounted on Allied planes during the D-Day invasion of France.

Throughout the 1940s, Devol continued to work on ideas that eventually led to a patent application for a magnetic recording system that controlled machines and the first industrial robot. He also worked on the team that developed the first commercial microwave and the Speedy Weeny machine, which automatically cooked and dispensed hotdogs. By the early 1950s, he was developing business applications for his magnetic recording system and developing high-speed printing systems.

In 1961, Devol's patent for a programmed article transfer was approved. The patent states that "the present invention relates to the automatic operation of machinery, particularly the handling apparatus, and to automatic control apparatus suited for such machinery." This invention, called the Unimate, changed the way companies looked at production lines. Instead of human hands, they turned to mechanical arms.

The first mechanical arm went into use at a General Motors plant in New Jersey, where it lifted and stacked hot metal parts. That machine weighed four thousand pounds and cost $25,000. Today, various types of mechanical arms can be seen working in thousands of businesses around the world. In 2005, Devol's Unimate was named one of the Top 50 Inventions of the Past 50 Years in *Popular Mechanics* magazine, and in 2011 Devol was inducted into the National Inventors Hall of Fame. Devol died on August 11, 2011, in Connecticut. He was ninety-nine years old.

\<History of Robots/\>

1495: Italian Leonardo da Vinci designs the first humanlike robot.

1727: The word *android* is entered in the *Chambers Cyclopedia*. It references German philosopher and alchemist Albertus Magnus's attempt to create a machine that resembles a human being.

1899: Serbian American Nikolai Tesla demonstrates the first remote-controlled vehicle. His boat can go, stop, submerge, turn left and right, and turn its lights off and on.

1920: The word *robot* is first used—in a science-fiction play written by Czechoslovakian playwright Karel Capek.

1926: Marie, a female robot, appears in the movie *Metropolis*.

1938: Americans Willard Pollard and Harold Roselund design a programmable paint-spraying mechanism.

1941: Isaac Asimov, American author and biochemistry professor, uses the term *robotics* to describe the technology that creates a machine with human intelligence.

1948: British robotics pioneer William Grey Walter creates the first turtle robots, named Elmer and Elsie. They mimic lifelike behavior using very simple circuitry.

Video Games for the Blind

Games developed for the blind or visually impaired are growing in popularity. They are produced using a technique called binaural recording. Binaural recording uses two microphones to record 3-D stereo sound that mimics the way the ear hears natural sound. Each scene in the game is recorded using this method, so the player is immersed in a realistic, surround-sound, audio-only experience.

The player wears headphones to listen to the noises within their virtual world and locate their position. Then, they use the touch screen on their mobile phone to control their character and navigate through each level.

In 2010, British game studio Somethin' Else released *Papa Sangre* and similar games. In 2014, French Dowino studio released *Blind Legend*. These and other video-less games are meeting a gaming need within the global market of 285 million blind or visually impaired people. The need for the same technology is growing within the app market as well.

According to Nathan Edge, a twenty-year-old blind gamer from Mansfield, England, "It [being blind] can be a very isolating world sometimes. You want to do the things other people are doing and playing. It gives you something to talk about with your friends. I can't play any of the text-based video games . . . I came across Papa Sangre II at the weekend and I can't stop playing it."[3]

1954: The first programmable robot, called UNIMATE, is designed by American inventor George Devol.

1956: The world's first robot company, Unimation, is formed by George Devol and Joseph Engelberger.

1961: UNIMATE, the first industrial robot, goes online at a General Motors factory in New Jersey. By obeying step-by-step commands stored on a magnetic drum, it handles hot die-cast metal parts.

1963: The Rancho Arm is created. It is the first robotic arm to be controlled by a computer. It has six joints that give it some of the function of a human arm.

1965: The first expert system is designed. It is called DENDRAL, and it knows everything about chemical analysis. DENDRAL can make decisions and solve problems faster than a human organic chemist.

1970: Shakey, the first mobile robot controlled by artificial intelligence, is introduced. It uses a television camera, laser range finder, and bump sensors to collect data. The data is sent to a computer, and the computer sends back commands that move Shakey at 6.5 feet per hour.

1974: The Silver Arm, controlled by a mini-computer, performs small-parts assembly using information it gets from touch-and-pressure sensors.

1979: The Stanford Cart crosses a chair-filled room without human assistance. It is able to judge distances between objects and avoid them.

1981: Japanese computer scientist Takeo Kanade builds a direct drive arm that has motors in its joints, which make it faster and more accurate than earlier robotic arms.

1989: Genghis is introduced. It is a walking robot created by the Mobile Robots Group at MIT. The unique way it moves is called the "Genghis gait."

1993: Monsieur is developed by Seiko Epson. It is the world's smallest robot and is certified by the Guinness Book of World Records.

1994: Dante II travels into the crater of Mount Spurr in Alaska. Its mission is to sample volcanic gases.

1996: RoboTuna, a robotic fish, is built by David Barrett at MIT. It is used to study how fish swim.

Gastrobot, a robot that digests food, is created. It converts food into carbon dioxide and carbon dioxide into power. It is given the nickname "flatulence engine," and later it's called Chew Chew.

1997: The first RoboCup football tournament is held in Nagoya, Japan. And the Pathfinder Mission lands on Mars. Its robotic rover, Sojourner, rolls down a ramp and onto Martian soil in early July. It continues to broadcast data from the Martian surface until September.

1998: Mindstorms, the robotics invention toy, is released by LEGO. Furby is released by Tiger Electronics at Christmastime. It is a toy that reacts to its environment and can speak about eight hundred English phrases.

2000: The United Nations estimates that there are 742,500 industrial robots in use worldwide. More than half are being used in Japan.

2001: The Space Station Remote Manipulator System (SSRMS) is successfully launched into orbit and begins building the International Space Station.

2002: ASIMO is the first robot that can walk independently and climb stairs. It is the first robot to ring the opening bell at the New York Stock Exchange.

2004: Epson releases the Micro Flying Robot, the world's smallest robotic helicopter. It weighs 0.35 ounces and is 2.8 inches in height. And Roomba sells its one millionth robotic vacuum.

2005: According to the International Federation of Robotics, the global market for intelligent service robots is expected to be $2.2 billion.

2007: The US Department of Defense, Defense Advanced Research Projects Agency's (DARPA) Grand Challenge includes robotic cars that compete in simulated city environments.

2020: It is predicted, by Japan's Mitsubishi Research Institute, that by this year, each household will own at least one robot.

Cybersecurity Coders

Programmer (noun):
A machine that turns coffee into code.

If you listen to the news, even once in a while, you know that internet security is the number-one challenge for your generation of computer users. You shop, bank, socialize, and work online, all with the understanding that your information is being kept safe. Safe from those who would steal your identity, take your money, destroy your reputation, or rip off your company's patents or your government's secrets. There are a myriad of ways that cybercriminals can raise havoc in peoples' lives. The coders who work to keep them away are cyber superheroes!

Jobs in cybersecurity fall into two broad categories, those who keep information safe by choosing the right software and systems for companies, and those who write the code that the first group relies on.

Those who write the code do so in several ways. First, they can put security measures into the initial code they write. Second, they can patch security breaches that cybercriminals find after the software is released. Third, they can write separate security programs that monitor systems and keep criminals from ever entering the system in the first place. And finally, they can work in teams to find and patch security weak spots before the hackers get a chance to find them.

Working as a cybersecurity coder is not a job you get right out of school. Security coders have a firm understanding of computer systems and have the ability to write code in multiple languages. If you get cybersecurity training, you can look forward to a well-paid, fairly secure career. The Bureau of Labor Statistics says that cybersecurity jobs will grow by 37 percent from 2012 to 2022.

As long as there is an internet, there will be cybercriminals. And as long as there are cybercriminals, there will be a need for talented coders to thwart them.

On July 20, 1969, the first man walked on the moon thanks to a smart, young coder named Margaret Hamilton. She headed the team that wrote the guidance software for the Lunar Module Eagle. At the time, firmware was written using core rope memory, where wires are wrapped around or through metal cores in a specific way that stores code in binary language (1s and 0s). If the wire goes through the core, it represents a 1. If the wire wraps around the core, it represents a 0. This coding was woven by hand, and it was tedious, time-consuming work. With amazing fore-thought, Hamilton's code saved the moon landing. When the computer started to overload with data, she was able to tell the computer to drop unneces-sary tasks, an ability that she wove into the code before Apollo 11 left Earth.

Name: Ryan McCrystal
Age: 12
Job (when not studying!): Cyber Sleuth and CyberPatriot
VII National Winner

When did you first discover that you were interested in writing code?

In fourth grade, when my computer teacher introduced me to Scratch, a drag-and-drop programming code. That year, I got the academic computer award in computer class. Later, in fifth grade, I joined a Greenfoot Java programming club. In sixth grade, we built and programmed LEGO Mindstorm robots using ROBOTC. I competed in the robotics event at the Virginia State Science Olympiad competition using a LEGO EV3 robot. At the last quarter of the year, I built toys in Autodesk Inventor, a 3-D model creator.

How did you learn to write code, and what language(s) do you know?

I learned to write code at school and then mostly from the internet. I know TI-BASIC, which is used to program a graphing calculator. This helped me get my math homework done fast. I also know ROBOTC, which is used for programming robots. I know some Java and Python at a basic level.

Describe the programs you have written or worked on.

One of the programs I made was in Greenfoot Java. I made a game where you had to catch sheep with a paddle and avoid catching the bombs. You get a point each time you catch a sheep, and lose ten points when you catch the bomb. Another program

I made was on my graphing calculator to help me with my math homework. I programmed it so it knew how to solve equations that I have to do over and over again, manually, like solving the Pythagorean theorem. I love making programs that help me get work done faster.

How did you first become interested in cybersecurity and decide to enter the CyberPatriot Program?

I learned about CyberPatriot (UScyberpatriot.org) from a STEM (Science, Technology, Engineering, and Mathematics) symposium we had at our school. It looked interesting to me, and I decided to try out one of the exhibition problems. After trying out the exhibition problem, I decided to create a CyberPatriot team after I discovered it was so fun.

Describe your journey through the CyberPatriot Program and competition.

Cybersecurity was a new concept for me. I found it to be fun, and I thought it would be an exciting career. I first read through the training modules to help get familiarized with the Cyber-Patriot Program and all of the things you need to be aware of in order to secure a computer from outside hostile intrusion. Some of the information in the training modules was new to me, but some was familiar to me, like adding and deleting user accounts, having virus protection, and setting up a firewall.

I learned the basics about CISCO Networking and how business computers are linked into a global network and also about securing multiple versions of Linux and Windows operating systems. The competition sessions were intense and the hours long, but they were so fun! The competition felt like a game, and the better we did, the more points we got. I got lots of experience working with my four teammates, and we got really good at problem solving under a deadline.

From September through March of sixth grade, Cyber-Patriot was my main extracurricular activity. The program goes through twelfth grade, and I definitely plan to be competing in CyberPatriot every year until I graduate high school in the Class of 2021. My younger brother, James, wants to be on a team with me when we're both in high school.

Describe the day of the national competition and how it felt to win.

Along with around twenty-five other middle school and high school CyberPatriot teams, we competed at the Gaylord National Conference Center located close to Washington, DC, for the CyberPatriot VII National Finals competition.

On the day of the middle school competition, my team and I were ready to go! Beyond setting up the security settings for all the computers and setting up critical services, part of the competition required the thwarting of a live penetration team attempting to invade our network. The one time they managed to sneak in, they left a funny note that popped up on the desktop. It said, "The Red Team Was Here!" We also had to keep web servers up. The red team was trying to make the servers go down. The longer we kept the services up, the more points we got. It was four hours long and so fun.

The second part of the middle school finals was a digital forensics challenge, which was totally new to our team. We searched a pretend office for digital crime evidence and tried to piece together what digital crime had taken place by looking at files on hidden flash drives. We had only ten minutes to figure it out! Digital forensics is a new and growing field in criminology, and this was new to us too. I think we might do better next year because we have a better idea of what to expect.

At the end of competition day, we were excited because we knew we had done the best we could. The following evening, at the awards ceremony, hearing my team's name called out as the winning team was not a huge surprise to me. It was like a big sigh of relief. We had worked hard to earn the national title, and we came to win it. I definitely want to do it again next year.

Besides the actual competition, we did some new things at national finals, like going on a field trip to Northrop Grumman in McLean, Virginia, to learn about digital forensics and managing big data. We toured moveable command centers made from railroad cars that had big monitors and blue lighting. We also met detectives who investigate cybercrime, as well as managers responsible for security from companies like Facebook.

Why do you think it's important that your peers learn how to write code and then get involved in cybersecurity?
Cybersecurity is an exciting career path for me, and I keep hearing that it needs more people with skills working in it. At the national finals, they kept telling us how important it is that we pursue jobs in that industry. That's why the Air Force Association developed CyberPatriot and created a way for kids my age to learn about cybersecurity and actively do it. Anyone can try it out and you don't need to do it at school. I think other kids who try it will like it too!

How do you balance your schoolwork with all your other activities?
I make sure I do my schoolwork first, and I don't sign up for more than I can handle. I like having free time to do whatever I feel like, like watching YouTube tech channels.

Where do you see yourself in ten years?
Graduating from college and then either working at Northrop Grumman designing security systems or starting my own cyber-security company.

0100100100100100100100100100100100100100010

<How Does Cybercrime Occur?/>
⇨ Through unpatched software

⇨ Through a Trojan (non-self-replicating malicious code) entering a user's system

⇨ Through phishing attacks—70 percent of all emails are spam, and malicious code is downloaded when a user clicks on an attachment

Staying Safe Online

Personal information about your offline life should never be shared online. This includes any information that someone can use to rob your house, ruin your reputation, or hack into your computer. Here's a list of information that should never be shared about you, your relatives, or your friends. Remember: If in doubt, then *don't* share. Always ask a trusted adult if you have any questions.

1. Full name and age

2. Telephone number and email address

3. User names or passwords

4. ID numbers and social security numbers

5. Where you live, including city or neighborhood

6. Where you work or go to school

7. Credit card numbers

8. License plate numbers

9. Places near where you live like restaurants, parks, and stores

10. If you are home alone or when you might be home alone

11. Names of your pets (*never* use a pet's name in any password)

12. Photos or videos that might reveal any of the above information (pictures of your house that show the street name or house number, pictures of your car that show the license plate)

13. Any picture or video that you wouldn't let Grandma see—remember, your future employer may find it while googling you

- ⇨ Through network-traveling worms (malicious code that replicates itself and spreads to other computers)

- ⇨ Through spearphishing, when multiple employees are sent emails that contain a Trojan attachment, which infects the entire company once one employee is tricked into clicking on the attachment

 # `<Spotlight/>`

Henry Edward "Ed" Roberts (1941–2010), Father of the Personal Computer

Henry Roberts was born in Miami, Florida on September 13, 1941. During his high school years, he was fascinated by electronics and built a relay-based computer. But his great passion was medicine. He entered the University of Miami with every intention of going to medical school and becoming a doctor. While there he met a neurosurgeon who shared his interest in electronics and convinced him to change his major to electrical engineering.

While still in college, Roberts married Joan Clark. When the first of their six children was born, the twenty-year-old dropped out of school and enlisted in the US Air Force, hoping to finish his degree under the Airman Education & Commissioning Program. Because of his electrical engineering background, he worked as an instructor at the Air Force's Cryptographic School in San Antonio, Texas. To supplement his income, he took on several different projects. The most interesting one was when he designed the electronics that animated Christmas characters in the windows of Joske's Department Store.

In 1968, Roberts finally finished his electrical engineering degree at Oklahoma State University and was sent to the Laser Division of the Weapons Laboratory at Kirtland Air Force Base in New Mexico. That same year, at the age of twenty-seven, he tried to get into medical school, but was told that he was too old.

Discouraged but not defeated, Roberts turned his attention back to electronics. He started his own company, Micro Telemetry Instrumentation Systems, and began building equipment for model-rocketry hobbyists and, later, kits for building an electronic calculator, something that was very high-tech and expensive at the time.

In 1973, competition from other manufacturers forced him to turn his company's attention toward building a programmable computer. On December 19, 1974, the company released the Altair 8800, a personal computer with an Intel 8080 microprocessor. It sold as a kit for $439 and assembled for $621. Within six months, the company had sold over five thousand computers, and the personal computer revolution began.

In 1977, Roberts sold his company and started a vegetable farm. A few years later, he entered Mercer University School of Medicine. When he finished residency, he settled down in rural Georgia and became a small-town doctor. In a 2001 article in the *New York Times* he said, "I think I'm making a fairly substantial contribution here. Maybe not to the wider world, but I think what I do now is important."[1]

Roberts died on April 1, 2010, after a monthlong battle with pneumonia. His contributions earned him the title of Father of the Personal Computer, but his lifelong dedication to rural medicine earned him a spot in many people's hearts. Roberts was also the first person to coin the term *personal computer*.

<Types of Cyberattacks/>

A cyberattack is an attack from one computer to another computer or to a website. The main goal is to gather information, including personal identities, credit card information, social security numbers, or bank account numbers. Here is a list of some of the more common types of attacks that coders work to prevent. Often they appear after you have downloaded software from the internet. All of these attacks are illegal and fall under the umbrella of cybercrime. The people who commit these attacks are cybercriminals.

⇨ Brute-Force Attack: Using a computer program, attackers search through all possible combinations of letters, numbers, and symbols to find your password.

⇨ Denial-of-Service Attacks: Attackers send a high volume of traffic or data through a specific server until the system gets overloaded (and causes a denial of service). When this happens, the attackers may find a way to enter the system.

⇨ Dictionary Attack: Using a computer program, attackers use every possible combination of words in the dictionary to find your password. This type of attack led to the need to put symbols and numbers into passwords.

⇨ Malware: Attackers write computer code to destroy something on a computer or steal private information.

⇨ Password Attack: Attackers focus on cracking your user name and password combinations.

⇨ Phishing. Malicious links in an electronic communication that attempt to steal your username, passwords, and credit card or bank account information.

⇨ Spyware: This type of malware sits on a computer and spies on users. It can collect each keystroke and steal private information like passwords.

⇨ Viruses: Computer code that infects a computer, can hide anywhere, and can replicate itself. Viruses survive by attaching themselves to programs or files.

⇨ Worms: Like viruses, they can replicate themselves. Unlike viruses, they don't need to attach themselves to a file or program. They can survive by themselves. They are much more dangerous than viruses. The most widespread worm is the Conficker, which has infected almost nine million computers.

⇨ Zero-Day Exploits: These happen when a hacker finds a security breach before the coders do. There are zero days between the time when the breach is found and when the system is first attacked.

Time-Triggered Viruses

Sometimes hackers create viruses that enter a computer and then sit and wait for a specific time to attack. Here are some famous time-triggered virus attacks.

⇨ The Jerusalem virus is one of the oldest and most common viruses around. It destroys data on an infected computer's hard drive every Friday the 13th.

⇨ The Michelangelo virus activates on March 6 (the anniversary of Michelangelo's birth in 1475), and overwrites all data on the hard disk with random characters, making recovery of any data unlikely.

⇨ The Chernobyl virus activates on April 26 (the anniversary of the Chernobyl Nuclear Power Plant meltdown), and wipes data from hard drives and overwrites the computer's BIOS chip, making the computer unusable.

⇨ The Nyxem virus wipes out an infected computer's files on the third of every month.

Name: Mark Armstrong
Job: Senior iOS engineer, eBay, Inc.

When did you first become interested in writing computer code and decide to make it the focus of your career?

I always enjoyed working with computers and took my first stab at programming when I was in elementary school, writing games in a programming language called BASIC on our family computer (an Amstrad with a whopping 128K of memory). Through middle school and high school, I didn't really do much coding. After graduating high school, I started doing some freelance graphic design. Along with that came the opportunity to put together some websites, so I dabbled with HTML and PHP a bit. It wasn't until the first iPhone came out that I really rediscovered my love for coding.

What education/work path did you take to get to your current position?

When the iPhone was introduced in 2007, I lived next to a good friend named John Marr. He and I were so enamored with the device and how much we could do with it, we had to find a way to be involved. At the time, there was no app store, so your only options were to develop web apps or apps that would run on jailbroken phones [phones that are modified so apps, other than those sold by Apple, can run on them]. Thankfully, by 2008, Apple opened up the iPhone to third-party developers, and that's when we were able to really dive in.

We started a company called SavageApps with a software engineer friend of ours named John Kent. He taught us many of the principles and practices used in software engineering that have served both of us well to this day. We released a number of apps, trying to see what people would be interested in. Ideas we thought were cool, and things we could do with the skills and resources we had.

Before long, one of our apps (iAmBeatBox) was featured by Apple on the front page of the app store. Our download numbers shot up from about two hundred per month to seventy thousand per day. The app was a free app, but we earned (barely) enough revenue from the advertising in the app to allow me to jump in with both feet and start working at the company full-time.

We continued to release updates and new applications over the next couple years. Eventually, for the sake of my wife and family, who had put up with quite a bit to allow me to pursue SavageApps, I decided to start looking for a job. That's when I landed at eBay. I interviewed with a number of companies and received a job offer from a start-up in San Francisco, but I wasn't especially keen on moving to the Bay Area. eBay's mobile department was right there in Portland, Oregon, and after a long day of interviews with half a dozen of their engineers, I was offered a position. I've spent the better part of three years at eBay and continue to learn and grow. The learning never stops. The landscape is always changing in the world of tech, and if you're not moving forward, you'll find yourself rapidly falling behind.

Why did you choose to write applications, and what type of applications do you write?
A fascination with the iPhone got me into it. I love to create, and there's nothing quite like taking an idea from nothing and turning it into something that millions of people use around the world. The move to mobile apps opened up a whole world of possibilities for software engineers that just didn't exist before. When I worked on SavageApps, we wrote mostly apps that tried to make creating music possible for even the least musical people out there. We created a number of other non-music-based apps, but the music apps were our bread and butter. When I started at eBay, I worked on an app called eBay Kleinanzeigen (it means

"classifieds"). I was the only engineer in the United States working with a team based out of Berlin. I did that for about a year, then started working on the main eBay iPad app and eventually moved over to the iPhone team.

Describe the process you go through to write an application.
There are many aspects to creating an application, and although it is a repetitive process, you have to start somewhere. Typically, you need some sort of design, and by design, I mean UX [user experience] design: how the app will look, function, et cetera. Often this takes the form of wireframes or sketches that may not be the final design but give the engineers an idea of what we're setting out to build.

From there, we come up with a design for the implementation. Now here, I'm talking about software design. Software design has to do with deciding how the app will actually be put together. What UI [user interface] elements will need to be built? What components need to exist to support those elements? What relationships will need to exist between all of these elements? How will they communicate? How will persistent data be handled throughout the app? And the list goes on.

A good software engineer probably spends more time thinking than typing. A well-thought-out and carefully implemented solution will save countless hours of work down the road and help ensure a more robust app and enjoyable experience for the end users.

From there, we start coding. Then, it's just a whole lot of writing code, evaluating, testing, and revising. Eventually, the app gets to a place where it can be played with and tested. As engineers finish up their work, the QA [quality assurance] team starts testing the app, and beta users get an early look at the app. The feedback received from the QA team and beta testers is funneled back through project managers to engineers who fix any bugs or implement suggested improvements. Of course, in the case of a small team like we had at SavageApps, the engineers double as the project managers and QA. Not ideal, but you make do with what you've got! When it comes to mobile application development, you're never really done. As soon as one version of the app is released (or sometimes a little before), you're onto the next release working on improvements, updates, and bug fixes.

What does an average workday look like for you?
Most software engineers are given a fair amount of flexibility with their schedule. Some like to get started early and finish up in time to go pick up the kids after school. Others work best late into the evening and don't make their way into the office until a bit later. When starting out on a new project, there are typically a number of meetings to attend. The engineer needs to be present to provide feedback from a technical perspective as to what's realistic and estimate the amount of work involved for any given task.

Once the project is kicked off, we usually have a daily "stand-up" meeting where everyone involved in the development process shares what they've been working on, what they'll be working on, and whether they're blocked on anything. Aside from the occasional meetings here and there, the rest of my time is spent architecting solutions for new features, coding those features, fixing bugs, or reviewing other people's code.

We use a system called pull-requests where an engineer requests changes to be pulled into the code base, and another engineer (or two) reviews those changes and either provides feedback or approves the request. That does take up a fair amount of time but helps keep simple oversights and mistakes from potentially causing big problems down the road. I'll take an occasional break to go play some foosball with the guys down the hall or grab a cup of coffee, but most of my time is spent at my desk in front of my computer or at a whiteboard. It's not for everyone, but that's the way I like it!

What do you see in the future for computer programming careers?
I think we're really just scratching the surface of what's possible in mobile. I also see trends in robotics and artificial intelligence that I don't see slowing down anytime soon. What's more, with wearables and the so-called Internet of Things, the demand for

skilled software engineers just continues to grow. I can't predict the future, but it's hard to see how pursuing a career in computer science wouldn't continue to lead to a lot of great opportunities as the tech landscape continues to evolve.

Do you have any tips for kids who are interested in becoming coders?

Do it! Just pick a language and start playing with it. There are so many resources available for free or at low cost online for those who want to learn! Take the computer science classes available to you, for sure, but don't settle for that. Play! Experiment! Explore! If you ask me, the best way to learn is by doing. Programming is one of those rare areas where given the desire, a computer, and an internet connection, you can really learn a lot. What's more, if you decide to learn how to build web applications in Ruby on Rails or try your hand at writing mobile applications for iOS or Android, it takes only time and a little determination to give it a shot. You might discover it's not really for you, but then again, you may completely fall in love with it.

0100100100100100100100100100100100100100100010

Hacktivist

A hacktivist is an individual or a group who breaks into a computer system to raise awareness for a political issue or a social cause. Although many people may agree with their motives, their actions are still considered criminal.

Here are a few hacktivist groups.

1. **Anonymous:** This is the most recognized movement. To call them a group or an organization would be misleading, because they have no known formal structure. Anonymous is a movement of hackers who may or may not work together. Members working under the Anonymous

banner have targeted financial institutions like PayPal and MasterCard, altered Twitter accounts and websites of groups like ISIS, and caused DDOS (distributed denial-of-service) attacks against the Chinese government in support of prodemocracy protesters. Officials in various countries, including the United States, the United Kingdom, Australia, the Netherlands, Spain, and Turkey, have arrested dozens of involved hackers but haven't managed to stop the attacks. Because there is no known leader, stopping Anonymous will prove difficult, if not impossible. They won *Time* magazine's poll for the 100 Most Influential People of 2012, though some wonder if they fixed the poll.

2. **Lulzsec:** Lulzsec was a black-hat hacking group of six people that formed around May 2011 from members of the Anonymous hacking movement. Their leader, Hector Monsegur, was arrested in June 2011. All but one of the others were arrested by September of that year. After his arrest, Monsegur used his skills to help the FBI identify major cybercriminals throughout the world and prevented at least three hundred cyberattacks.

3. **Lizard Squad:** The Lizard Squad is another black-hat hacking group that has mainly targeted gaming networks, including Xbox Live and the PlayStation network.

Hackers, the Government, and Cyber Warfare

After years of referring to cyber warfare as something found in the plot of a novel or a science-fiction movie, governments around the world are waking up to the potential national security threat posed by cyberattacks. Countries like China and Iran have huge numbers of hackers dedicated to penetrating the computer infrastructure of the United States, Europe, and other countries they see as potential enemies. Their goal is to destroy power grids, steal company secrets, sabotage

First Computer Virus

The first far-reaching, self-replicating virus designed to infect a personal computer was written by Richard Skrenta. When he was thirteen, he got an Apple II computer for Christmas, and he said, "It took over my life. I spent every waking hour immersed in computer games and programming."[1]

In 1982, after a few attempts to play jokes on his friends by infecting their floppy disks, Skrenta decided to see if he could create a program that would spread by itself. He designed the Elk Cloner virus to infect a computer from a floppy disk. Once uploaded, the virus would run, undetected, in the background, waiting patiently to infect any new floppy disks that were inserted. When the infected disk was removed and inserted into another computer, that computer harbored the virus and also infected any new floppy disks. In this way, the virus hopped from disk to disk, spreading itself from computer to computer.

"At the time I thought it was hysterically funny," said Skrenta. The virus posted taunting messages from Skrenta after every five boots from the disk; then, after the fiftieth boot, it displayed this text:

```
Elk Cloner: The program with a personality
It will get on all your disks It will
    infiltrate your chips Yes it's Cloner!
It will stick to you like glue It will modify
    ram too Send in the Cloner!
```

The virus didn't cause any real harm to the computer, but it spread quickly and alerted computer owners around the world to how vulnerable computers were to outside hackers, both friend and foe. "It worked like a charm," said Skrenta. "And spread all over the place."

Today, one of the most widespread viruses is the Conficker Virus, which has infected almost nine million computers.

financial institutions, derail trains, and melt down nuclear power plants.

They are looking for a way to create havoc. According to President Barack Obama in his 2013 State of the Union address, "America must also face the rapidly growing threat from cyberattacks . . . We cannot look back years from now and wonder why we did nothing in the face of real threats to our security and our economy."[2]

Although the government needs hackers to stay on top of this new cyber warfare, companies are spending a lot more money on cybersecurity (estimated at over $86 billion in 2016). They are willing to pay higher wages than the government to get the best talent. And companies have less strict rules about dress codes, criminal history, tattoos, and work practices. For these reasons, the government has a difficult time filling their positions, let alone hiring the best hackers. The National Cybersecurity and Communications Integration Center monitors threats to US computers, including NASA and the IRS. Their top priority is to change their image so they can attract younger, talented coders. They are promoting a sense of patriotic duty and emphasizing the benefits of getting high-level security clearance.

A new entry into cyber warfare is the entrepreneurial hacker. They hunt for security flaws, and when they find one, they sell it to whichever government—like Russia, North Korea, or the US National Security Agency (NSA)—is willing to pay. Companies like Google and Microsoft also pay for the information hackers find. Getting the technical details of a single vulnerability from a hacker can cost as much as $150,000.

The following are areas that are both important to us and susceptible to attack. Attacks that have already happened prove that companies and our government must stay alert:

⇨ **Federal Government:** The largest theft of information happened to the United States government when two major breaches of their databases occurred in 2014. The personal information of 22.1 million people—mainly federal employees, contractors, and their families and friends—was stolen. The breaches are linked to the Chinese government.

⇨ **Nuclear Power:** Stuxnet was a worm or virus that infected Iran's nuclear centrifuges. Iran hasn't confirmed whether it did any lasting damage, but an employee said a second attack caused the song "Thunderstruck" to play throughout the plant.

> ⇨ **Electric Grid:** A 2013 congressional report on electric grid vulnerability said that more than a dozen utility companies had reported frequent cyberattacks. One company had more than ten thousand cyberattacks in a month.

⇨ **Trains:** In 2008, a fourteen-year-old created a device that caused four trains to jump their tracks. In 2011, hackers disrupted train signals in the Pacific Northwest for two days.

⇨ **Water Systems:** In 2011, hackers burned out a water pump in Springfield, Illinois, and another hacker discovered a three-letter password that let him gain access to a water plant in Houston, Texas.

⇨ **Satellites:** Satellites were hacked in 2007 and 2008. Depending on the type of satellite, this could cause disruption of internet service or military operations.

⇨ **Stock Market:** On April 23, 2013, at 1:07 PM, the Syrian Electronic Army hacked into the Associated Press (AP) and tweeted that the White House had been bombed and President Obama was injured. The stock market temporarily lost $200 billion.

⇨ **Large Companies:** In 2013, Target announced that hackers had stolen over forty million debit and credit card numbers and the personal information of around 110 million people. Cost to Target: over $250 million.

⇨ **Health Insurance Companies:** In 2015, hackers stole the personal information of about eighty million Anthem Health Insurance customers. The information included their social security numbers and birthdates, information that is commonly used to steal individual identities.

⇨ **International Banks:** In 2014, contact information for over eighty-three million households and small businesses was stolen from JP Morgan Chase. This happened despite the fact that they spent $250 million on cybersecurity that year.

⇨ **Human Error:** Experian, a national credit reporting agency, accidentally sold millions of Americans' personal information to a scam artist in Vietnam. That person posted the information to a database that was accessed by criminals more than three million times.

⇨ **Entertainment Companies:** On November 24, 2014, a group called the Guardians of Peace hacked into Sony's database and stole emails and other private information. The FBI linked the group to the North Korean government. The attack was in retaliation for a movie Sony was about to release about an assassination attempt on the North Korean president. Sony was also attacked in 2011 and seventy-seven million credit card account numbers were stolen, mostly through the Sony PlayStation network.

Wearing a Hacker's Hat

Back-hat hackers attack computer security for malicious reasons or for personal gain. They are the ones you see portrayed in movies and on television. They steal, destroy, or change data to make a network unusable. They are also called "crackers," and they don't share their knowledge of security breaches with anyone. What they do is illegal.

White-hat hackers are ethical computer hackers or computer security experts. They are the coders who specialize in ways to test systems to find vulnerabilities. White-hat hackers often work for the government. What they do is legal.

Gray-hat hackers sit in an area between the black and white hackers. They surf the internet, looking for vulnerabilities. When they find one, they contact the administrator and offer to share or correct their find for a fee. What they do is still considered illegal and unethical.

Resources

Learn to Code Online

App Inventor: appinventor.org
Blocky Games: blockly-games.appspot.com
Code: code.org.
CodeHS: codehs.com
Code Academy: codeacademy.com
Code Avengers: codeavengers.com
CodeCombat: codecombat.com
Code Monkey: playcodemonkey.com
Code Monster, Code Maven, Game Maven, Data Maven:
   crunchzilla.com
Gamestar Mechanics: gamestarmechanic.com
Girls Learn Code: girlslearncode.com
Hackety Hack: hackety.com
Kahn Academy: khanacademy.org
Lightbot: lightbot.com
Made w/ Code: madewithcode.com
Scratch: scratch.mit.edu
Stencyl: stencyl.com
Tynker: tynker.com

Apps for iPhone or iPad

Cargo-Bot: twolivesleft.com/CargoBot
Daisy the Dinosaur: daisythedinosaur.com
Hopscotch: gethopscotch.com
Move the Turtle: movetheturtle.com

Apps for Android

Hackasaurus
Hakitzu Elite: Robot Hackers
Run Marco!
TinyTap Make & Play

Competitions

Air Force Association's CyberPatriot—The National Youth Cyber
   Education Program: uscyberpatriot.org
American Computer Science League: acsl.org
First Lego League (Grades 4-8): usfirst.org/roboticsprograms/fll
First Robotics Competition (Grades 9-12) usfirst.org/robotics
   programs/frc
First Tech Challenge (Grades 7-12): firstinspires.org/robotics/fll
GamesByTeens: gamesbyteens.org
High School Capture the Flag: hsctf.com
Internet Problem Solving Contest: ipsc.ksp.sk
USA Computing Olympiad: usaco.org
Zero Robotics: zerorobotics.mit.edu

Classes, Clubs, and Camps

Black Girls Code: blackgirlscode.org
Coder Dojo: coderdojo.com

Digital Medial Academy: digitalmediaacademy.org
Emagination Computer Camps: computercamps.com
Girls Who Code: girlswhocode.com
iDTech: idtech.com
Kids, Code, and Computer Science magazine: kidscodecs.com
LEGO Robotics Programs: usfirst.org/roboticsprograms/fll
National Computer Camps: nccamp.com
Programming 4 Girls: programming4girls.com
Tera Byte Video Game Creation Camp: terabytegames.com/
Tech Trek!: aauw.org/what-we-do/stem-education/tech-trek
YMCA Summer Technology Camps: contact your local YMCA
#YesWeCode: yeswecode.org

Books

C++ for Kids: A Fun and Visual Introduction to the Fundamental Programming Language by Blaise Vanden-Heuvel and John C. Vanden-Heuvel Sr.

Hello App Inventor!: Android Programming for Kids and the Rest of Us by Paula Beer and Carl Simmons

Hello Raspberry Pi!: Python Programming for Kids and Other Beginners by Ryan Heitz

Hello World!: Computer Programming for Kids and Other Beginners by Warren Sande and Carter Sande

JavaScript for Kids: A Playful Introduction to Programming by Nick Morgan

Learn to Program with Scratch: A Visual Introduction to Programming with Games, Art, Science, and Math by Majed Marji

PHP and MySQL for Kids: A Playful Introduction to Programming by Johann-Christian Hanke

Python for Kids: A Playful Introduction to Programming by Jason R. Briggs

Ruby for Kids For Dummies by Christopher Haupt

Ruby Wizardry: An Introduction to Programming for Kids by Eric Weinstein

Video Game Programming for Kids by Jonathan S. Harbour

Glossary

algorithm. A formula or set of steps for solving a particular problem. To be an algorithm, a set of rules must be specific and have a clear stopping point.

analytical. Using analysis or logical reasoning to break a problem into its essential parts or basic principles.

application. Software program written to perform a specific task. When installed on a device, it runs inside the operating system until it is closed. Applications are called "apps" when they are installed on a mobile device.

artificial intelligence. The branch of computer science concerned with making computers behave like humans. The term was coined in 1956 by John McCarthy.

binary. Pertaining to a number system that has just two unique digits.

calculate. To determine or ascertain by mathematical methods; compute.

circuit. Another name for a chip, an integrated circuit (IC) is a small electronic device made out of a semiconductor material.

coder. A person who writes computer code.

compiler. A computer program that translates a program written in a high-level language into another language, usually machine language.

CSS. Cascading Style Sheets. A new feature being added to HTML that gives both website developers and users more control over how pages are displayed.

cyber. A prefix used in a growing number of terms to describe new things that are being made possible by the spread of computers.

data. Distinct information that is formatted in a special way. Data exists in a variety of forms, like text on paper or bytes stored in electronic memory.

database. Often abbreviated DB, it is basically a collection of information organized in such a way that a computer program can quickly select desired pieces of data. You can think of a database as an electronic filing system.

debug. The process of identifying and removing errors from computer hardware or software code.

deploy. To install, test, and implement a computer system or application.

digital. Any system based on discontinuous data or events. Computers are digital machines because at the basic level, they can distinguish between just two values, 0 and 1.

domain. A group of computers and devices on a network that are administered as a unit with common rules and procedures, defined by the IP (internet protocol) address within the internet.

downlink. In satellite communications, it is the establishment of a communications link from an orbiting satellite down to one or more ground stations on Earth.

electronics. The science dealing with the development and application of devices and systems involving the flow of electrons in a vacuum, in gaseous media, and in semiconductors.

entrepreneur. A person who organizes and manages any enterprise, especially a business, usually with considerable initiative and risk.

hardware. Objects that you can actually touch, like disks, disk drives, display screens, keyboards, printers, boards, and chips.

host. To store a website or other data on a server or other computer so that it can be accessed over the internet.

hypertext. A special type of database system in which objects (text, pictures, music, programs, and so on) can be creatively linked to each other.

integrated. A popular computer buzzword that refers to two or more components merged together into a single system. For example, any software product that performs more than one task can be described as integrated. Increasingly, the term *integrated software* is reserved for applications that combine word processing, database management, spreadsheet functions, and communications into a single package.

internet. A global network connecting millions of computers. More than 190 countries are linked into exchanges of data, news, and opinions.

internet of things. All the objects—from appliances to mobile phones—which are given unique identifiers and can be connected to the internet by sensors or devices that allow them to send and receive data.

IP. Internet protocol. A set of rules governing the format of data sent over the Internet or other network.

ISP. Internet service provider. A commercial, community-owned, nonprofit, or privately owned group that provides services for accessing, using, or participating in the Internet.

lexicon. The vocabulary of a particular computer language.

logical. Reasoning or capable of reasoning in a clear and consistent manner.

microprocessor. A silicon chip that contains a central processing unit (CPU). In the world of personal computers, the terms *microprocessor* and *CPU* are used interchangeably.

modem. Hardware that allows a computer to transmit information over telephone lines in what is called a dial-up connection.

motherboard. The main circuit board of a microcomputer. The motherboard contains the connectors for attaching additional boards.

multithreading. The ability of a program or an operating system to manage its use by more than one user at a time and to manage multiple requests by the same user without requiring that multiple copies of the program be running on the computer.

patch. Also called a fix. A quick repair to a software program that fixes a problem until a permanent solution can be found and written for the next version.

portfolio. The group of applications that show an individual's computer programming skills.

program. An organized list of instructions that, when executed, causes the computer to behave in a predetermined manner. Without programs, computers are useless.

programmer. An individual who writes programs or a device that writes a program onto a PROM (programmable read-only memory) chip on which data can be written only once.

query. A request for information from a database. There are three general methods for posing queries: choosing parameters from a menu, query by example, and query language.

RAM. Random-access memory.

ROM. Read-only memory.

script. Another term for macro or batch file, a script is a list of commands that can be executed without user interaction.

ship. A computer program that is complete and ready for download or for purchase.

software. Computer instructions or data. Anything that can be stored electronically is software. The storage devices and display devices are hardware.

subprogram. A part of a program that can be designed and tested independently.

subroutine. A section of a program that performs a particular task.

symmetrical multiprocessing. The processing of programs by multiple processors that share a common operating system and memory. The processors share memory and the I/O bus or data path. A single copy of the operating system is in charge of all the processors.

tag. A command inserted in a document that specifies how the document, or a portion of the document, should be formatted.

transistor. A device composed of semiconductor material that amplifies a signal or opens or closes a circuit.

update. A minor release or version upgrade to an existing software product that adds minor features or corrects problems.

uplink. In satellite communications, uplink is the establishment of a communications link from a ground station up to the orbiting satellite.

URL. Uniform resource locator. It is the global address of documents and other resources on the World Wide Web.

vacuum tube. An electron tube from which almost all air or gas has been evacuated; formerly used extensively in radio and electronics.

validation. Verification that something is correct or conforms to a certain standard.

webcomic. An online comic strip or cartoon, especially one that was originally published online.

white space. Spacing is any section of a document that is unused or space around an object. White spaces help separate paragraphs of text, graphics, and other portions of a document. It helps a document look less crowded and makes it easier to read.

ACKNOWLEDGMENTS

My thanks to Andrea for her hard work helping me research this book and for keeping a sense of humor as we struggled to understand this interesting, but foreign to us, subject.

And thanks to Arden for his patience in explaining difficult concepts and to Paul for his coding expertise. You helped make this manuscript as accurate as possible. Your help was invaluable, but any mistakes rest solely with me.

NOTES

Chapter 1
1. *CBS News*, "Merging Traditional Toys with Artificial Intelligence," February 17, 2015, http://www.cbsnews.com/news/anki-ceo-boris -sofman-on-future-of-toys-robotics-new-york-city-toy-fair.

2. James B. Meigs, "Inside the Future: How PopMech Predicted the Next 110 Years," *Popular Mechanics*, December 10, 2012, http:// www.popularmechanics.com/technology/a8562/inside-the-future -how-popmech-predicted-the-next-110-years-14831802.

Chapter 2
1. "Summary of Source Data for Code.org Infographics and Stats," Code.org, accessed July 22, 2015, https://docs.google.com /document/d/1gySkItxiJn_vwb8HIIKNXqen184mRtzDX 12cux0ZgZk/pub.

2. The Ada Project, "Pioneering Women in Computing Technology: Sister Mary Kenneth Keller," School of Computer Science Carnegie Mellon University, accessed July 22, 2015, https:// www.women.cs.cmu.edu/ada/Resources/Women/#Sister%20 Mary%20KennethKeller.

3. Lizzie Widdicombe, "The Programmer's Price," American Chronicles, *The New Yorker*, November 24, 2014, http://www .newyorker.com/magazine/2014/11/24/programmers-price.

4. Cory J. Miller, *Essential Career Advice for Developers: 10 Keys to Happy, Prosperous Work* (Edmond, OK: iThemes Media, 2013), https://ithemes.com/wp-content/uploads/downloads/2013/09/Essential-Career-Advice-For-Developers-Ebook.pdf.

Chapter 3
1. Chris Kite, "How Coding Works." Code Conquest, accessed July 22, 2015, http://www.codeconquest.com/what-is-coding/how-does-coding-work.

Chapter 4
1. "USS Hopper (DDG 70) 'Amazing Grace,'" *America's Navy*, accessed July 22, 2015, http://www.public.navy.mil/surfor/ddg70/Pages/namesake.aspx#.VbKn_PkQjHp.

2. "Input & Output: The Mouse," Computer History Museum, accessed July 22, 0215. http://www.computerhistory.org/revolution/input-output/14/350.

3. Peter Wayner, "12 Predictions for the Future of Programming," *JavaWorld*, February 3, 2014, http://www.javaworld.com/article/2093747/java-ios-developer/12-predictions-for-the-future-of-programming.html.

Chapter 5
1. "Mobile Technology Fact Sheet," Pew Research Center, October 2014, http://www.pewInternet.org/fact-sheets/mobile-technology-fact-sheet; "Majority of US Internet Users to Use a Connected TV by 2015," *eMarketer*, June 13, 2014, http://www.emarketer.com/Article/Majority-of-US-Internet-Users-Use-Connected-TV-by-2015/1010908; Barry Levine, "Americans Don't Yet Own Many Smart Appliances—But They're about To (report)" *Venture Beat*, September 1, 2014, http://venturebeat.com/2014/09/01/report

-americans-are-adopting-the-Internet-of-things; "Planet of the Phones," *The Economist*, February 28, 2015, http://www .economist.com/news/leaders/21645180-smartphone-ubiquitous -addictive-and-transformative-planet-phones.

Chapter 6
1. Paul Krill, "IT's Most Wanted: Mainframe Programmers," *InfoWorld*, December 1, 2011, http://www.infoworld.com/article /2618174/it-training/it-s-most-wanted--mainframe-programmers .html.

Chapter 7
1. Harrison Jacobs, "Pro Gamer Describes the Difference Between Playing in the US and Korea—the Mecca of Video Game," *Business Insider*, May 16, 2015, http://www.businessinsider.com/league-of -legends-christian-rivera-talks-about-pro-gaming-in-korea-2015 -5#ixzz3aco4jrLh.

2. Drew Liming and Dennis Vilorio, "Work for Play: Careers in Video Game Development," *Occupational Outlook Quarterly*, Fall 2011: 3.

Chapter 8
1. "Total Number of Websites & Size of the Internet as of 2013," Factshunt.com, accessed July 22, 2015, http://www.factshunt.com /2014/01/total-number-of-websites-size-of.html.

Chapter 9
1. Alexander C. Kaufman, "Google Is Putting Its New Self-Driving Cars on the Road," *The Huffington Post*, May 15, 2015, http://www .huffingtonpost.com/2015/05/15/google-self-driving_n_7291218 .html.

2. A. M. Turing, "Computing Machinery and Intelligence," *Mind* 59 (1950): 433–60, Loebner.net, accessed July 10, 2015, http:// loebner.net/Prizef/TuringArticle.html.

3. Claire Brennan, "'Video-less' 3D Games Developed for Blind Players," *BBC News*, August 19, 2014, www.bbc.com/news /technology-28757186.

Chapter 10

1. Stephen Miller, "PC Pioneer Inspired Microsoft Founders," *Wall Street Journal*, April 13, 2012, http://www.wsj.com/articles/SB10001 424052702304871704575159680960424558

2. John Leyden, "The 30-Year-Old Prank that Became the First Computer Virus," *The Register*, December 14, 2012, http://www .theregister.co.uk/2012/12/14/first_virus_elk_cloner_creator _interviewed/.

3. Siobhan Gorman, "Executive Order Seeks Safer Cyber Networks," *Wall Street Journal*, February 12, 2013, http://www.wsj .com/articles/SB10001424127887323511804578300601262155388.

BIBLIOGRAPHY

Websites

Bureau of Labor Statistics: bls.gov

Code: code.org

ENIAC Programmers Project: eniacprogrammers.org

Hackerspaces: wiki.hackerspaces.org

Hour of Code: hourofcode.com/us

Institute for the Certification of Computing Professionals: iccp.org

Internet Movie Database: imdb.com

RobotWorx: A Scott Technology Ltd. Company: robots.com

Tech Terms: techterms.com

X2 Biosystems: x2biosystems.com

Articles

"5 Basic Elements of Game Design," Make School, accessed June 1, 2015, https://www.makeschool.com/gamernews/298/5-basic -elements-of-game-design.

"A Short History of Robots," Rover Ranch, accessed June 2, 2015, http://prime.jsc.nasa.gov/ROV/history.html.

"A Wearable Pioneer: Hubert W. Upton of Bell," IEEE International Symposium on Technology and Society, January 7, 2013, http://veillance.me/blog/2013/1/7/a-wearable-pioneer -hubert-w-upton-of-bell.

"Ada Byron, Countess of Lovelace," The San Diego Supercomputer Center: Women in Science, accessed February 27, 2015, http:// www.sdsc.edu/ScienceWomen/lovelace.html.

Almendrala, Anna. "Scientists May Have Just Found a Solution for Deadly Superbugs," *Huffington Post*, May 7, 2015, http://www .huffingtonpost.com/2015/05/07/antibiotic-resistance-software _n_7228766.html.

"Animation Programmers and Engineers Creative and Passionate," *Software Engineer Insider*, accessed May 1, 2015, http://www.software engineerinsider.com/careers/animation-programmer-engineer .html#.VT6m7ZMQjHo.

"Anonymous Wins Time Magazine Poll for Most Influential Figure," *Examiner*, April 1, 2012, http://www.examiner.com/article /anonymous-wins-time-magazine-poll-for-most-influential-figure.

Anthony, Sebastian. "Could You Hack Into Mars Rover Curiosity?" ExtremeTech.com, August 13, 2012, http://www .extremetech.com/extreme/134334-could-you-hack-into-mars -rover-curiosity.

Beck, Kent. *Test Driven Development: By Example*. Boston: Addison Wesley Professional, 2002.

Bennet, Tom. "Frozen." Bennet.org, July 2014, http://bennet.org /blog/frozen.

Bentley, Mark. "Software Upgrade at 655 Million Kilometres," European Space Agency, March 28, 2013, http://blogs.esa.int /rosetta/2014/03/28/software-upgrade-at-655-million-kilometres.

"Bill Gates." Biography.com. Accessed May 11, 2015. http://www .biography.com/people/bill-gates-9307520.

Bratcher, Emily H. "Web Developer," *U.S. News and World Report*, accessed May 11, 2015, http://money.usnews.com/careers/best-jobs /web-developer.

Brennan, Claire. "'Video-less' 3D games developed for blind players," *BBC News*, August 19, 2014, http://www.bbc.com/news /technology-28757186.

"Clearing Up Confusion: Deep Web vs. Dark Web," BrightPlanet .com, March 17, 2014, http://www.brightplanet.com/2014/03 /clearing-confusion-deep-web-vs-dark-web.

Cohodas, Marilyn. "Why We Need Better Cyber Security: A Graphical Snapshot," *InformationWeek*, November 28, 2014, http:// www.darkreading.com/operations/why-we-need-better-cyber -security-a-graphical-snapshot-/d/d-id/1317398?image_number=1.

"Common Deep Web and Big Data Questions Answered—Part 1," BrightPlanet.com, November 24, 2015, http://www.brightplanet .com/2014/11/common-deep-web-big-data-questions-answered -part-1.

"Computer Basics: Understanding Applications," GCF Global, accessed May 11, 2015, http://www.gcflearnfree.org /computerbasics/3.

"Computer Designer: Job Description, Duties and Requirements," Study.com, accessed April 2, 2015, http://study.com/articles /Computer_Designer_Job_Description_Duties_and _Requirements.html.

"Computer History," Computer Hope, accessed May 11, 2015. http://www.computerhope.com/history.

"Computer Programmer," IT Career Finder, accessed March 3, 2015, http://www.itcareerfinder.com/it-careers/computer -programmer.html.

"Computer Programmers," Bureau of Labor Statistics, January 8, 2014, www.bls.gov/ooh/computer-and-information-technology /computer-programmers.htm.

"Computer Virus Statistics," Statistic Brain Research Institute, April 28, 2015, http://www.statisticbrain.com/computer-virus-statistics.

"Could Sony hack happen to more corporations?" *CBS News*, April 10, 2015, http://www.cbsnews.com/news/could-sony-hack-happen -to-more-corporations.

Cuthbertson, Anthony. "Charlie Hebdo Paris massacre: Anonymous vows to avenge victims with cyber-war on jihadists," *International Business Times*, January 9, 2015, http://www.ibtimes.co.uk/charlie -hebdo-paris-massacre-anonymous-vows-avenge-victims-cyber -war-jihadists-1482675.

David, Leonard. "Best Ways to Learn Programming for Beginners," Leo Pixel, February 10, 2015, http://www.leopixel.com/2015/02 /10-best-ways-to-learn-programming-for.html.

Dfordsi. "Web Designer vs. Web Programmer vs. Web Developer," Strategic Insights Brand Marketing, December 15, 2009, http://www.strategicinsights.net/tech-questions/web-designer -vs-web-programmer-vs-web-developer.

DiLascia, Paul. "What Makes Good Code Good?," *MSDN Magazine*, July 2004, pg. 144, www.literateprogramming.com /quotes_dd.html.

"Doug's 1968 Demo," Doug Engelbart Institute, accessed May 11, 2015, http://www.dougengelbart.org/firsts/dougs-1968-demo.html.

Dredge, Stuart. "Coding at School: A Parent's Guide to England's New Computing Curriculum," The Guardian, September 4, 2014, http://www.theguardian.com/technology/2014/sep/04/coding -school-computing-children-programming.

Eadicicco, Lisa. "What the People Who Worked on Google Glass Think of Microsoft's Crazy New Holographic Computer," *Business Insider*, May 9, 2015, http://www.businessinsider.com/google-glass -hololens-2015-5#ixzz3acjtNPbm.

Estes, Adam Clark. "What Is 'the Cloud'—And Where Is It?" Gizmodo.com, January 29, 2015, http://gizmodo.com/what-is-the -cloud-and-where-is-it-1682276210.

Ferretti, Matt. "5 Top Video Games for Kids," *ConsumerReports*, December 8, 2014, http://www.consumerreports.org/cro/news /2014/12/5-top-video-games-for-kids/index.htm.

Finley, Klint. "Obama Becomes First President to Write a Computer Program," *WIRED*, December 8, 2014, http://www .wired.com/2014/12/obama-becomes-first-president-write -computer-program.

Finley, Klint. "What Exactly Is GitHub Anyway?," TechCrunch. com, July 14, 2012, http://techcrunch.com/2012/07/14/what -exactly-is-github-anyway.

Foster, Peter. "'Bogus' AP tweet about explosion at the White House wipes billions off US markets," *The Telegraph*, April 23, 2013, http://www.telegraph.co.uk/finance/markets/10013768/Bogus -AP-tweet-about-explosion-at-the-White-House-wipes-billions -off-US-markets.html.

Fox-Brewster, Thomas. "DoD, Yahoo Hack Suspects and Alleged Lizard Squad Member Arrested By UK Cops," *Forbes*, March 6, 2015, http://www.forbes.com/sites/thomasbrewster/2015/03/06 /dod-yahoo-and-lizard-squad-hacker-suspects-arrested-by-uk-cops.

Fronczak, Tom. "Top 20 Most Essential Software for Artists and Designers," *Animation Career Review*, September 4, 2013, http:// www.animationcareerreview.com/articles/top-20-most-essential -software-artists-and-designers?page=0,0.

Gallagher, Sean. "Hackers Promise 'Christmas present' Sony Pictures won't like," Arstechnica.com, December 14, 2014, http:// arstechnica.com/security/2014/12/hackers-promise-christmas -present-sony-pictures-wont-like.

Gates, Bill. "About Bill," *Gatesnotes: The Blog of Bill Gates*, accessed July 10, 2015, http://www.gatesnotes.com/globalpages/bio.

Geiling, Natasha. "RoboCup: Building a Team of Robots That Will Beat the World Cup Champions," *Smithsonian Magazine*, June 8, 2014, http://www.smithsonianmag.com/innovation/robocup -building-team-robots-will-beat-world-cup-champions -180951713/?no-ist.

"GGJ 2015: The Official Stats," Global Game Jam, Inc., accessed May 1, 2015, http://globalgamejam.org/news/ggj-2015-official -stats.

Goldman, David and Jose Pagliery. "The Worst Hacks of All Time," Cable News Network, June 5, 2015, http://money.cnn.com /gallery/technology/2015/02/05/worst-hacks-ever/4.html.

Goldstein, Matthew, Nicole Perlroth, and Michael Corkery. "Neglected Server Provided Entry for JPMorgan Hackers," *New York Times,* December 22, 2014, http://dealbook.nytimes.com/2014 /12/22/entry-point-of-jpmorgan-data-breach-is-identified/.

Goodfellow, Chris. "The Startup Developing a Revolutionary Bionic Hand," *Business Zone,* April 8, 2015, http://www .businesszone.co.uk/topic/business-profiles/startup-developing -revolutionary-bionic-hand/59865.

Greelish, David. "Remembering Ed Roberts," *The Classic Computing Blog,* October 10, 2012, http://www.classiccomputing. com/CC/Blog/Entries/2010/10/10_Remembering_Ed_Roberts .html.

Greengard, Samuel. "A Brief History of the Internet of Things," *Baseline Magazine,* September 24, 2014, http://www.baselinemag .com/networking/slideshows/a-brief-history-of-the-internet-of -things.html.

Grimes, Roger A. "The 5 Cyber Attacks You're Most Likely to Face," *InfoWorld,* December 4, 2012, http://www.infoworld.com /article/2616316/security/the-5-cyber-attacks-you-re-most-likely -to-face.html?page=2.

Guo, Philip. "Python Is Now the Most Popular Introductory Teaching Language at Top U.S. Universities," *Communications of the ACM,* July 7, 2014, http://cacm.acm.org/blogs/blog-cacm/176450 -python-is-now-the-most-popular-introductory-teaching -language-at-top-us-universities/fulltext.

Handlos, David. "Computer Information Systems vs Computer Science," Get Educated, accessed March 3, 2015, http://www

.geteducated.com/careers/521-computer-information-systems-vs
-computer-science.

Hemmendinger, David. "Computer Programming Language," *Encyclopedia Britannica*, January 27, 2015, http://www.britannica
.com/EBchecked/topic/130670/computer-programming-language.

Hidalgo, Jason. "10 Best Kids' Video Games of 2014," *USA Today*,
December 23, 2014, http://www.usatoday.com/story/tech
/gaming/2014/12/23/best-video-games-2014/20796723.

Higgins, John. "Code-Writing Clicks as Kids Get Creative," *Seattle
Times*, May 18, 2014, http://www.seattletimes.com/seattle-news
/code-writing-clicks-as-kids-get-creative.

History.com Staff. "The Invention of the Internet," A+E Networks,
accessed May 11, 2015, http://www.history.com/topics/inventions
/invention-of-the-internet.

"How Big Is the Internet?," BrightPlanet.com, November 5, 2015,
http://www.brightplanet.com/2014/11/big-internet.

"How to Become a Video Game Designer: Education and Career
Roadmap," Study.com, accessed April 24, 2015, http://study.com
/articles/How_to_Become_a_Video_Game_Designer_Education
_and_Career_Roadmap.html.

"International Programmer's Day," Time and Date AS, accessed
February 27, 2015, http://www.timeanddate.com/holidays/world
/international-programmers-day.

"Introduction to Web Development," Code Conquest, accessed
April 3, 2015, http://www.codeconquest.com/what-is-coding
/web-programming.

Janssen, Cory. "Artificial Intelligence (AI)," *Techopedia*, accessed
May 11, 2015, http://www.techopedia.com/definition/190
/artificial-intelligence-ai.

Jacobs, Harrison. "Pro Gamer Describes the Difference Between
Playing in the US and Korea—the Mecca of Video Games,"
Business Insider, May 16, 2015, http://www.businessinsider.com
/league-of-legends-christian-rivera-talks-about-pro-gaming-in
-korea-2015-5.

Jacobs, Ryan. "A Brief History of Awesome Robots: From
Futuristic Cities to a 1980s Chinese Restaurant, a Peek Back at the
Real and Fictional Robot Icons of the Last Century," May 13, 2013,
http://www.motherjones.com/media/2013/05/robots-modern
-unimate-watson-roomba-timeline.

Kar, Aditi. "Lady Ada Lovelace and the Analytical Engine,"
University of Oxford Mathematical Institute, accessed February 27,
2015, http://people.maths.ox.ac.uk/kar/AdaLovelace.html.

Kaufman, Alexander C. "Google Is Putting Its New Self-Driving
Cars on the Road." *Huffington Post*, May 15, 2015, http://www
.huffingtonpost.com/2015/05/15/google-self-driving_n_7291218
.html.

Kite, Chris. "5 Personality Traits Every New Programmer Should
Have," Learn to Code with Me, September 18, 2014, http://
learntocodewith.me/posts/5-computer-programmer-personality
-traits.

"Konrad Zuse," Encyclopedia.com, accessed April 24, 2015, http://
www.encyclopedia.com/topic/Konrad_Zuse.aspx.

Kosner, Anthony Wing. "Developers in Demand: Platform as a Service Is Key to Growth of Mobile Cloud Computing," *Forbes*, June 8, 2012, http://www.forbes.com/sites/anthonykosner/2012 /06/08/developers-in-demand-platform-as-a-service-is-key-to -growth-of-mobile-cloud-computing.

Kramer, Miriam. "Philae Spacecraft Landed 3 Times on Speeding Comet: See Its First Photos," Space.com, November 13, 2014, http://www.space.com/27761-philae-comet-landing-bounces-first -photos.html.

Krill, Paul. "IT's Most Wanted: Mainframe Programmers" *InfoWorld*, December, 2011, http://www.infoworld.com /article/2618174/it-training/it-s-most-wanted—mainframe -programmers.html.

Kushner, David. "Geeks on the Front Lines," *Rolling Stone*, September 11, 2013, http://www.rollingstone.com/feature/the -geeks-on-the-frontlines#i.otmxhhikqegqts.

Leyden, John. "The 30-year-old prank that became the first computer virus." *The Register*, December 14, 2012, http://www.theregister .co.uk/2012/12/14/first_virus_elk_cloner_creator _interviewed.

Liming, Drew and Dennis Vilorio. "Work for Play: Careers in Video Game Development," Bureau of Labor and Statistics, accessed June 23, 2015, http://www.bls.gov/careeroutlook/2011/fall/art01. pdf.

"List of Programming Languages for Artificial Intelligence," Wikipedia.org, last modified on July 7, 2015, http://en.wikipedia .org/wiki/List_of_programming_languages_for_artificial _intelligence.

"LulzSec Hacker Helps FBI Stop over 300 Cyber Attacks," *BBC News*, May 26, 2014, http://www.bbc.com/news/technology -27579765.

Manrique, Victor. "35 Inspiring Game Examples for Gamification Mechanics," EpicWinBlog.net, June 27, 2013, http://www .epicwinblog.net/2013/06/35-inspiring-game-mechanics-examples .html.

Martinson, Kelly J. "Abacus," Encyclopedia.com, accessed February 23, 2015, http://www.encyclopedia.com/topic/abacus.aspx.

Matthews, Dylan. "Meet Margaret Hamilton, the Badass '60s Programmer Who Saved the Moon Landing," Vox.com, May 30, 2015, http://www.vox.com/2015/5/30/8689481/margaret-hamilton -apollo-software.

McCormick, Kristen and Michael R. Schilling. "Animation Cels," The Getty Conservation Institute, accessed May 1, 2015, http:// www.getty.edu/conservation/publications_resources/newsletters /29_1/animation.html.

"Merging Traditional Toys with Artificial Intelligence," *CBSNews*, February 17, 2015, http://www.cbsnews.com/news/anki-ceo-boris -sofman-on-future-of-toys-robotics-new-york-city-toy-fair.

Miller, Daniel. "Software Behind 'Big Hero 6' Pushes Envelope on Computer Animation," *LA Times*, February 20, 2015, http://www .latimes.com/entertainment/envelope/cotown/la-et-ct-disney -animation-big-hero-6-20150220-story.html#page=1.

Miller, Stephen. "PC Pioneer Inspired Microsoft Founders," *Wall Street Journal*, April 3, 2012, http://www.wsj.com/articles/SB100014 24052702304871704575159680960424558.

"Most Widely Used Programming Language (for Games)," GameDev.net, September 17, 2013, http://www.gamedev.net /topic/647957-most-widely-used-programming-language-for -games.

Nakashima, Ellen. "22.1 Million Compromised in Government Database Breaches," *Washington Post*, July 9, 2015, http://www.washingtonpost.com/rweb/politics/federal-authorities-security-clearance-system-hack-affected-215-million-people/2015/07/09/03e99927f875ede051966589e7138b52_story.html.

Nakashima, Ellen and Andrea Peterson. "Report: Cybercrime and Espionage Costs $445 Billion Annually," *Washington Post*, June 9, 2014, https://www.washingtonpost.com/world/national-security/report-cybercrime-and-espionage-costs-445-billion-annually/2014/06/08/8995291c-ecce-11e3-9f5c-9075d5508f0a_story.html.

"Non-English-Based Programming Languages," *Wikipedia.org*, last modified on June 15, 2015, http://en.wikipedia.org/wiki/Non-English-based_programming_languages.

Nusair, David. "Animated Film Timeline," About.com, accessed May 1, 2015, http://movies.about.com/od/animatedmovies/a/history-animated-films.htm.

Pinola, Melanie. "Which Programming Language Should I Learn First?," *LifeHacker*, December 5, 2013, http://lifehacker.com/which-programming-language-should-i-learn-first-1477153665.

Rouse, Margaret. "Zero-day exploit," Search Security, accessed April 17, 2015, http://searchsecurity.techtarget.com/definition/zero-day-exploit.

Savitz, Eric. "How You Can Use the Cloud for Rapid-Fire Innovation," *Forbes*, April 30, 2012, http://www.forbes.com/sites/ciocentral/2012/04/30/how-you-can-use-the-cloud-for-rapid-fire-innovation/2.

"Sister Mary Kenneth Keller," The Ada Project: Pioneering Women in Computing Technology, accessed June 2, 2015, http://www.women.cs.cmu.edu/ada/Resources/Women/#Sister%20Mary%20KennethKeller.

INTERNET

Smith, Dave. "There's One Glaring Problem with Oculus Rift's Plan to Conquer Virtual Reality," *Business Insider*, May 15, 2015, http://www.businessinsider.com/oculus-rift-wont-work-with-your -apple-computer-2015-5#ixzz3acyF7ZgW.

Soderbery, Rob. "How Many Things Are Currently Connected to the 'Internet of Things' (IOT)?," *Forbes*, January 7, 2013, http:// www.forbes.com/sites/quora/2013/01/07/how-many-things-are -currently-connected-to-the-internet-of-things-iot.

"Software Developers," Bureau of Labor Statistics, January 8, 2014, http://www.bls.gov/ooh/computer-and-information-technology /software-developers.htm.

Solimine, Andrew J. "The Future of Programming: 5 Reasons to Code in the Cloud." *Huffington Post*, July 22, 2014, http://www .huffingtonpost.com/andrew-j-solimine/the-programming -revolutio_b_5607587.html.

Soper, Taylor. "Analysis: The Exploding Demand for Computer Science Education, and Why America Needs to Keep Up," Geekwire.com, June 6, 2014, http://www.geekwire.com/2014 /analysis-examining-computer-science-education-explosion.

"St. Isidore of Seville," AmericanCatholic.org, accessed May 11, 2015, http://www.americancatholic.org/Features/Saints/saint .aspx?id=1343.

Starr, Michelle. "World's First 3D-Printed Apartment Building Constructed in China," *CNet Magazine*, January 19, 2015, http:// www.cnet.com/news/worlds-first-3d-printed-apartment-building -constructed-in-china.

Strassler, Matt. "The Trigger: Discarding All but the Gold," Of Particular Significance: Conversations About Science with Theoretical Physicist Matt Strassler, November 4, 2011, http://profmattstrassler.com/articles-and-posts/largehadroncolliderfaq/the-trigger-discarding-all-but-the-gold.

Strickland, Jonathan. "10 Worst Computer Viruses of All Time," Howstuffworks.com, August 26 2008, http://computer.howstuffworks.com/worst-computer-viruses.htm.

"Summary of Source Data for Code.org Infographics and Stats," Code.org, accessed February 27, 2015, https://docs.google.com/document/d/1gySkItxiJn_vwb8HIIKNXqen184mRtzDX12cux0ZgZk/pub.

Tabuchi, Hiroko. "$10 Million Settlement in Target Data Breach Gets Preliminary Approval," *New York Times*, March 19, 2015, http://www.nytimes.com/2015/03/20/business/target-settlement-on-data-breach.html.

"Terminology: What's a Co-op and What's an Internship?," Virginia Tech, January 16, 2013, http://www.career.vt.edu/coop/Terminology.htm.

"The Demo," Stanford University's MouseSite, accessed May 11, 2015, http://web.stanford.edu/dept/SUL/library/extra4/sloan/MouseSite/1968Demo.html?utm_source=twitterfeed&utm_medium=twitter.

"The Mouse," Computer History Museum, accessed April 24, 2015, http://www.computerhistory.org/revolution/input-output/14/350.

"The 100 Best Animated Movies: The Best CG Movies," *Time Out New York*, accessed May 1, 2015, http://www.timeout.com/newyork/film/the-100-best-animated-movies-cgi.

Tillman, Karen. "How Many Internet Connections Are in the World? Right. Now," Cisco.com, July 29, 2013, http://blogs.cisco.com/news/cisco-connections-counter.

"Timeline of Computer History," Computer History Museum, accessed May 11, 2015, www.computerhistory.org/timeline.

Tomlinson, Simon and Hannah Parry. "Hacker Group Anonymous Claims to Have Forced Their First Jihadi Website Down Since Announcing Online War Against Extremists in the Wake of Charlie Hebdo Murders," *Daily Mail*, January 12, 2015, http://www.dailymail.co.uk/news/article-2906987/Hacker-group-Anonymous-claims-forced-jihadi-website-announcing-online-war-against-extremists-wake-Charlie-Hebdo-murders.html.

"Top Ten Countries with Highest number of PCs," Maps of World, February 1, 2012, http://www.mapsofworld.com/world-top-ten/world-top-ten-personal-computers-users-map.html.

"Top 100 Animation Movies," Flixter, Inc., accessed May 1, 2015, http://www.rottentomatoes.com/top/bestofrt/top_100_animation_movies/?category=2.

"Top 75 Computer-Animated Movies," *Sky UK,* accessed May 1, 2015, http://www.sky.com/tv/channel/skymovies/gallery/the-ultimate-computer-toons.

"Total Number of Websites and Size of the Internet as of 2013," FactsHunt.com, January, 2014, http://www.factshunt.com/2014/01/total-number-of-websites-size-of.html.

"USS Hopper (DDG 70)," Navy.mil, accessed April 24, 2015, http://www.public.navy.mil/surfor/ddg70/Pages/namesake.aspx#.VTaQQJMQjHo.

Vaughan-Nichols, Steven J. "Six Clicks: The Six Fastest Computers in the World," ZDNet.com, November 20, 2014, http://www .zdnet.com/pictures/six-clicks-the-six-fastest-computers-in-the -world/5.

Wales, Michael. "3 Web Dev Careers Decoded: Front-End vs. Back-End vs. Full Stack," Udacity, Inc., December 8, 2014, http:// blog.udacity.com/2014/12/front-end-vs-back-end-vs-full-stack -web-developers.html.

Walker, Tom. "20 Most Popular Open Source Software Ever," *Tripwire Magazine*, May 19, 2013, http://www.tripwiremagazine .com/2010/03/20-most-popular-open-source-software-ever-2.html.

Wayner, Peter. "12 Prediction for the Future of Programming," JavaWorld.com, February 3, 2014, http://www.javaworld.com /article/2093747/java-ios-developer/12-predictions-for-the-future -of-programming.html?page=2.

Webster, Guy et al. "Mars Tugging on Approaching NASA Rover Curiosity," NASA, August 4, 2012, http://www.nasa.gov/mission _pages/msl/news/msl20120804.html.

Weiss, Todd R. "Google Introduces Kids to Coding Through Blockly Games Project," *eWeek*, August 17, 2014, http://www .eweek.com/it-management/google-introduces-kids-to-coding -through-blockly-games-project.html.

"When Was the First Computer Invented?," Computer Hope, accessed February 17, 2015, http://www.computerhope.com/issues /ch000984.htm.

"Who Invented the Internet?," Computer Hope, accessed May 11, 2015, http://www.computerhope.com/issues/ch001016.htm.

"Who Is the Father of the Computer?," Computer Hope, accessed February 20, 2015, http://www.computerhope.com/issues /ch001335.htm.

"Who Was Charles Babbage?," University of Minnesota College of Science and Engineering Charles Babbage Institute, accessed February 17, 2015, http://www.cbi.umn.edu/about/babbage.html.

Widman, Jake. "The Most Popular Programming Languages of 2015." NewRelic.com, July 7, 2015, https://blog.newrelic.com /2015/07/07/popular-programming-languages/.

Wigmore, Ivy. "Internet of Things," Whatis.com, June 2014, http://whatis.techtarget.com/definition/Internet-of-Things.

"World-Wide Internet Usage Facts and Statistics," Factshunt.com, January 2014, http://www.factshunt.com/2014/01/world-wide -internet-usage-facts-and.html.

Yandoli, Krystie. "High School Students Build Robotic Locker Opener for Classmate with Muscular Dystrophy (VIDEO)," *Huffington Post*, May 7, 2013, http://www.huffingtonpost.com/2013 /05/07/high-school-students-buil_0_n_3230214.html.

Zuse, Horst. "The Life and Work of Konrad Zuse," *EPE Online Magazine*, Wimborne Publishing Ltd and Maxfield & Montrose Interactive Inc., accessed July 21, 2015, https://web.archive.org /web/20090629003415/http://www.epemag.com/zuse.